JUDGE VICTORIA PRATT served as the chief judge of the Newark Municipal Court, is a professor at the Newark School of Criminal Justice, and has taught at the Rutgers School of Law. Her TED Talk clip, "How Judges Can Show Respect," has been viewed over thirty million times on Facebook. She lives in Montclair, New Jersey.

Conclusion: A Letter to My Son

1. Emma Jane Kirby, "How Norway Turns Criminals into Good Neighbours," BBC News, July 6, 2019, www.bbc.com/news/stories -48885846.

2. Stephen R. Covey, *The 7 Habits of Highly Effective People: Powerful Lessons in Personal Change* (New York: Fireside Press, 1989), 28.

PRAISE FOR *THE POWER OF DIGNITY*

"Judge Pratt's book is profoundly honest, compelling, and illuminating. It summons all of us, particularly people of conscience, to enact change in our communities."

—RYAN HAYGOOD, president and CEO,
New Jersey Institute for Social Justice

"*The Power of Dignity* is a profoundly important book written by a profoundly important advocate for restorative justice. Judge Pratt reimagines our justice system and offers an essential and timely narrative about the transcendent power of centering human dignity and the meaning of justice itself."

—DAHLIA LITHWICK, senior editor, *Slate*,
and host of the *Amicus* podcast

THE POWER OF DIGNITY

*How Transforming Justice
Can Heal Our Communities*

JUDGE
VICTORIA PRATT

Foreword by
Senator Cory Booker

SEAL PRESS
New York

Seal Press
Hachette Book Group
1290 Avenue of the Americas, New York, NY 10104
www.sealpress.com
@sealpress

Printed in the United States of America

First Edition: May 2022

Published by Seal Press, an imprint of Perseus Books, LLC, a subsidiary of Hachette Book
Group, Inc. The Seal Press name and logo is a trademark of the Hachette Book Group.

The Hachette Speakers Bureau provides a wide range of authors for speaking events.
To find out more, go to www.hachettespeakersbureau.com or call (866) 376-6591.

The publisher is not responsible for websites (or their content) that are not owned
by the publisher.

Print book interior design by Jeff Williams.

Library of Congress Cataloging-in-Publication Data
Names: Pratt, Victoria, author.
Title: The power of dignity: how transforming justice can heal our communities /
    Judge Victoria Pratt; foreword by Senator Cory Booker.
Description: New York, NY: Seal Press, [2022] | Includes bibliographical references.
Identifiers: LCCN 2021056788 | ISBN 9781541674837 (hardcover) | ISBN 9781541674820
    (ebook)
Subjects: LCSH: Criminal justice, Administration of—United States. | Respect for persons—
    Law and legislation—United States. | Fairness.
Classification: LCC HV9950 .P72 2022 | DDC 364.973—dc23/eng/20220105
LC record available at https://lccn.loc.gov/2021056788

ISBNs: 9781541674837 (hardcover), 9781541674820 (ebook)

LSC-C

Printing 1, 2022

*To my beloved mother, Elsa, thank you for giving
me everything I would need for my life's journey.
Que Dios me la bendiga.
To my awesome husband, Paul, and cherished son,
Hendrick, thank you for filling my life
with love, laughter, and light.*

Remember those in prison as if you were together with them in prison, and those who are mistreated as if you yourselves were suffering.

HEBREWS 13:3,
THE BIBLE, NEW INTERNATIONAL VERSION

CONTENTS

Foreword by Senator Cory Booker   1

Introduction   7

Chapter 1   A Better Approach   27

Chapter 2   I Hear You   59

Chapter 3   I See You   89

Chapter 4   Poverty Is Not a Crime   121

Chapter 5   Reforms That Transform   147

Chapter 6   Transforming the Justice System   183

Chapter 7   Reformed Leadership   217

Conclusion: A Letter to My Son   253

Author's Note   265

Acknowledgments   267

Notes   273

FOREWORD

Senator Cory Booker

The problems of our broken justice system are systemic, but its consequences—lives extinguished, families severed, futures stolen—are seen in individual lives and individual trauma. It is that focus on people that Judge Victoria Pratt brought to work every day in the courthouse. Before she arrived, many Newark residents had approached the courthouse with dread, referring to it as "The Green Monster."

The Green Monster. A place that eats people up: processing and punishing them—for one person, a fine they'll never be able to pay; for another, a stay in jail that will only exacerbate the problems that keep bringing them into the courthouse. There was little thought of hearing people's stories, let alone of offering a helping hand. That was just the way it was done.

But Victoria Pratt was determined to not be a typical part of the system. When, as mayor of Newark, I appointed her to the bench in 2009, I pointed out that this wasn't a role the founders had ever envisioned for a Latina, African American woman.

Judge Pratt was the daughter of an African American father and a mother who had emigrated from the Dominican Republic. As you'll read, there is plenty of research showing that Judge Pratt's approach from the bench works, but I'm willing to bet she learned as much about transforming the justice system at the Curly Comb, her mother's downtown beauty salon, as she did at Rutgers Law School.

Judge Pratt believes in meeting people where they're at. Newarkers are a proud and resilient people. Historically, the courts and government have failed to serve them in the manner they deserve. As mayor, I was determined to change that. For Judge Pratt, changing that culture meant treating everyone who came before her with respect. We all have an inherent dignity that can be convenient for the justice system to ignore. Her work meant trying to understand the whole person; no one is the worst thing they ever did, or is defined by their trauma, substance use, or poverty. It meant thinking of the justice system as a community-building, not community-corroding, institution. As Judge Pratt writes, how many opportunities to do good have we missed as a country because of our obsession with punishment?

A lot of this comes down to trust: Do we trust our justice system to be fair? Do we trust it to leaven consequences with mercy? Do we even trust it to keep us safe? As we saw in the great wave of protest against racist police violence that swept this country in 2020, the answer for more and more people is "no."

For many, it's been "no" for a very long time. When I took over as mayor of Newark in 2006, crime was at an apex, and trust in the institution of justice was at another low ebb. The dilapidated municipal courthouse was a symbol of that—piles of boxes with folders of individual cases overflowed into the hallways. Sitting in a courtroom watching people get arraigned one after the other, it could feel more like a factory. Head across the street for a cup of coffee, and you might hear people angrily dismissing the court as "only interested in taking our money."

The outcomes such an institution generates are the opposite of what people say they want. Untold sums of money are poured into a system that is very far from just and often only makes communities less safe. It imprisons the poor, the mentally ill, people with substance use disorders, survivors of trauma and sexual abuse, and above all Black and Brown people. It's a system that wastes what is every community's greatest natural resource: its people.

Attempting to fix this in Newark was not the work of a moment. Appointing Judge Pratt—someone who knew and felt accountable to the community she served—was part of that effort. Another milestone was the creation of Newark Community Solutions, New Jersey's first community court, and asking Judge Pratt to occupy its bench.

Created with the Center for Court Innovation—which had already pioneered similar successful courts in Manhattan and Brooklyn—Newark Community Solutions grew from a simple idea: what if, rather than seeing an opportunity for punishment, we saw someone's ending up in the criminal justice system as an opportunity to get that person help so they wouldn't end up in the same place again?

You will read the stories in this book: the father who needs help with his addiction so he can reconnect with his son; the homeless veteran who needs treatment and gets assistance from

Veterans Affairs through the court; the young man struggling with mental illness who is finally connected to a therapy and treatment program and gets his life on track.

Social workers, counselors, and community-based services make up the heart of Newark Community Solutions. Redirecting money from the justice system into alternative forms of community and social support was one of the central rallying calls of the 2020 protests. With its focus on treatment over jail, the community court movement—while remaining squarely part of the traditional system—arguably laid some of the groundwork for what blossomed into a more radical demand for alternatives.

Judge Pratt was one of the people who willed Newark Community Solutions into existence.

When she took over in "Part Two" Criminal Court, her new courtroom, nothing was in place—there were no community services, and court staff were hardly on board with the idea of adopting a new approach. Now, more than a decade since its founding, Newark Community Solutions has thrived, inside and outside the courtroom, building a deep presence in some of the city's most marginalized neighborhoods.

With community building as its North Star, the model has shown itself to be both adaptive and resilient. Newark Community Solutions is no longer only about working to solve problems once someone has shown up in court; at that point, many of the harms of system involvement, for both the individual and their community, have already begun. It's become a platform for community capacity building and collaboration—one that works on new responses to violence, for example, and new ways to help young people avoid the juvenile justice system.

When Judge Pratt was sworn in, I said, "She is a leader who could do anything." We're fortunate that she has chosen to dedicate herself to this work. As a daughter of Newark, she grants everyone's story significance.

The pandemic's corrosive path through this country has laid bare how unequal we still are as Americans, how much we are all connected, and what we owe to each other. To me, that's the message at the core of this book. If we heed it, it could transform more than our justice system.

INTRODUCTION

I have been called the judge of second chances. The truth is most of the people who appeared in my court never got a first chance. Many were lost on the wrong path long before they entered my courtroom. It was my goal to reverse the trajectory of those who appeared before me.

My mission and commitment to reform the criminal justice system has gained national and international acclaim. I've seen the ways the system traditionally operates, and too often it demeans and denigrates participants. Therefore, it engenders neither respect for nor compliance with the law. In contrast, my approach was human centered and respectful, ensuring that everyone maintained their dignity. During my tenure as the chief judge in Newark Municipal Court in Newark, New Jersey, I spent years gaining a deep understanding of how to deliver justice to court participants in a manner that redirected their behavior and increased their trust in the legal system.

While presiding over Newark Community Solutions, Newark's community court program, I used innovative problem-solving and procedural justice—a proven, evidence-based approach that increases the public's trust in the justice system. By providing alternative sentences to low-level offenders—including community service, counseling sessions, and my signature assignment of reflective essays—I was able to provide punishment with assistance. This respectful approach ensures that people are treated with dignity, and it has had a transformational impact on court participants, the community, and court practitioners.

In 2017, my TED Talk about my approach to justice, called "How Judges Can Show Respect," went viral globally. It has been translated into sixteen languages, and across social platforms it has reached over thirty-six million views. Thrive Global has featured it as one of the Top 15 Most Viral Motivational Talks on Facebook. I've brought my insights to the US Department of Justice and to jurisdictions across the nation. Internationally, I've traveled as far as Dubai, Ukraine, England, Scotland, Trinidad and Tobago, the Dominican Republic, and Mexico, facilitating workshops and presentations for judges, attorneys, and government officials.

Donning a black robe, I served in a courtroom usually crammed wall to wall with Black and Brown bodies. I watched the police lead the predominately Black prisoners, chained to one another, out of the cellblock and into the courtroom—dragging their feet as they attempted to walk in unison with handcuffs, accompanied by the deafening clanking sounds of the chains that bound them together. It was reminiscent of the captive Africans being led to the slave ships that ripped away their humanity and forced them to embark on the grim and murderous journey of the transatlantic slave trade. It's now the twenty-first century in the United States, and tragically the African captives' descendants' condition has not much changed.

Looking at the emaciated faces, the dirt-stained clothes, I tried to imagine what they would have achieved had their lives not been derailed—lives disrupted and ravaged by a long battle with addiction, years of trauma caused by sexual molestation, or war-related posttraumatic stress disorder, to name just a few of the life destroyers I've encountered in the justice system. Instead of adopting the traditional approach to justice that dehumanizes people, reducing them to mere labels as offenders or victims, I decided to make the courtroom a place that could both punish and heal. The traditional approach of severely punishing people for minor acts did not work and did little to improve outcomes—it only drove people deeper into the justice system. Not to mention, we were also choosing to punish them for their station in life. Dispensing justice in that manner felt unfair. In fact, the maxim that common sense is not that common plays out every day in our long-standing approach to justice.

Normally, minor contacts with the justice system result in major life disruptions and detours for low-level offenders. They would appear before me after being arrested on offenses such as loitering, shoplifting, trespassing, drug possession, and prostitution, to name a few of the charges. These charges soon became plea deals with exorbitant fines, fees, and penalties.

Witnessing this cookie-cutter approach to justice, I quickly realized it was ineffective and lacked humanity. But what if we meted out justice in a manner that made the courthouse a place of transformation?

When I was appointed as a judge of the Newark Municipal Court by then Mayor Cory Booker back in 2009, it wasn't considered a plum assignment. And when I was transferred to the Criminal Court Part Two, there were only two reactions: my colleagues either gave me their condolences or laughed heartily. As is true in many city courts, the churn of low-level cases into our courthouse felt relentless. In my early days on the job, I knew the work wasn't making a difference. Many of the defendants who appeared before me quickly became familiar faces. These were not hardened criminals. These were people serving life sentences, thirty, sixty, or ninety days at a time. I realized pretty quickly that the standard options available to judges, fines or jail, wouldn't help them with their problems.

I noticed something else from my vantage point on the bench. Many of the defendants didn't understand what was happening to them, and they didn't respect the court process. To be fair, they had little guidance on either count. They were dealing with an antiquated structure that appeared to be designed to keep them in the dark and cycling through the system. No one took the time to tell them how it worked or what was expected. When we spoke to defendants at all, we quite literally looked down on them—think of how the judge's bench is elevated above everyone in the courtroom.

How the system currently works is terrible for everyone—victims, police, defendants, judges—and for justice. A judge's job doesn't end with issuing a ruling. If the authority is experienced by the defendant as unfair coercion, it shouldn't be surprising when that ruling isn't obeyed. Distrust of the justice system then radiates from a defendant—to his family, his neighbors, colleagues, and eventually to entire communities.

This takes us into the heart of a lot of heated conversations and demonstrations occurring today. Discussions are happening throughout the country about our criminal justice system's incarceration rates and the unfair treatment of Black and Brown people and other vulnerable communities. I don't pretend to have the answers to all these problems, but I can tell you about what made a difference in my courtroom. It was the use of procedural justice—a simple approach to transforming our court system using the power of dignity and respect. It was ensuring that I saw people and their humanity, listened deeply to people, and understood the impact of poverty on the community and on its members' entry into the criminal justice system.

Detractors of my in-depth, respectful approach will attempt to shift our focus to how low-level defendants' acts of self-medicating violates our laws. They'll try to distract us from the glaring moral issue before us: Our criminal justice system is a wreck, and we must address and correct the larger problems that thrust people into it. Yes, we professionals in the justice system regularly witness others' human failings—however, our most significant impediment to tackling these issues is our refusal to confront *our own* failings.

I've often been asked how I became a crusader for justice. Truthfully, many small and connected lessons helped create my ideology and passion for justice.

Growing up, I watched white people take advantage of my working-class parents, and I felt embarrassed when I saw them forced to be deferential while they were being belittled. My parents, descendants of the transatlantic slave trade, landed in the Caribbean and North America, inheriting the painful legacy of opression. I realized that I had to fight for them and others like them who were targeted because of their race, poverty, accents, immigrant status, or other perceived disadvantages. As a young adult, I tried to find ways I could take on an advocacy role professionally. Before entering my senior year of college, I joined Literacy Volunteers of America. The training sessions were held at Rutgers Law School in Newark. As I walked through the building, I thought about the law graduates whose portraits were displayed in framed photographs in the hallways. *Why couldn't I attend and graduate from law school?* The only thing that was stopping me was fear. Hadn't every injustice I saw in my community already convinced me that I had to do more?

Later in my legal career, I served as Counsel to the Council President in Newark. In that role I met with constituents about the full range of their concerns. The most common issues often centered on unemployment, underemployment, high crime rates in their neighborhoods, lack of health insurance, a scarcity of affordable housing, and impending foreclosure. During this time, Cory Booker became mayor in a landslide electoral victory, ushering in a new era of progressive thinking in Newark. As I sat in on the hearings for new judges nominated by Mayor Booker, I thought, *The municipal court, the entry point to the courts. What an amazing opportunity to make an impact.*

This notion began my journey to becoming a judge. After some lobbying of council members, the corporation counsel, and the chief of staff, Mayor Booker decided to steal me away from the legislative branch and appoint me as the first judge of Dominican descent to the Newark Municipal Court. Councilman Ras Baraka, who later became mayor, would subsequently appoint me to serve as the court's chief judge.

This journey ultimately landed me at the Newark Municipal Courthouse at 31 Green Street. Residents had given the building the unaffectionate nickname "The Green Monster." Imagine that. The people who relied on this institution to dispense justice, fairness, equity, and restoration believed it to be a frightening, threatening creature with cruel intentions, recklessly inflicting great harm on those it captured.

But residents were right not to trust us. The Green Monster feasted on thousands of victims every year. People were arrested for minor infractions, charged, released, and rearrested for failure to appear and failure to pay. Situated above the city jail, the courthouse churned through its prey in a never-ending, revolving cycle of injustice. The city jail had also been ordered condemned years earlier due to its conditions, and numerous suicides occurred there while people were in police custody. During President Barack Obama's administration, the Newark Police Department was the subject of a US Department of Justice consent decree, which forced the department to correct its practices and protect its citizens' rights. A DOJ investigation found what Black residents already knew: that Black people in Newark made up 85 percent of unconstitutional pedestrian stops, even though they made up only 54 percent of the city's population. Black residents were more frequently stopped, frisked, and searched than their white and Latino counterparts. I became a judge in a climate where the public's trust in the judicial system was nonexistent.[1]

The distrust was well placed. We weren't delivering justice. Judges were reduced to ineffective bill collectors, imposing fines we knew would never get paid. The most vulnerable in the community routinely received quality-of-life tickets for having the audacity to exist when they could not afford housing. We were voyeurs observing the worst parts of their lives, and we punished them for their hardships. It was as if the Green Monster were lying in wait for people to make a mistake. As people went about their day, it seemed that justice system officials could leap out in a "gotcha" moment and swallow them whole.

How we currently deliver justice undermines confidence in our justice system and discourages the public from participating in or respecting the process—a process that is intended to hold up the existing order in society, when that social order crushes millions who have no path out of poverty. The justice system maintains the existing social, economic, and racial stratification in this country. When the people believe they are being subjected to a kangaroo court (a sham legal performance with no regard for justice or fairness), confusion, disillusionment, and antagonism reign, providing fertile soil for distrust to grow. This distrust is so prevalent in people of color that they won't seek available justice system resources for help. African Americans and Latinos are less likely than whites to call police to report disturbances or crime, even when there is a need for medical emergency services.[2]

We punish people for not respecting the legal process, but we fail to look at the underlying causes for that lack of respect. We fail to consider how our decisions and actions perpetuate and worsen existing inequality. We don't consider the long-lasting, far-reaching effects of unfairness in our institutions. A ruling for one person will have an immediate effect on their family and friends. Yet we rarely see or acknowledge the resulting damage those decisions have on people and their communities. For example, a marijuana conviction will prevent a father from obtaining gainful employment or volunteering at his child's school. Asking a person to return to court repeatedly to show proof of payment of fines may lead to them losing their job due to tardiness.

Judges, despite being overwhelmed with inundated court calendars, are expected to dispense justice promptly and concisely. They are not given the time or the resources to fully consider the cases before them, much less to help the defendants with their underlying struggles, which range from insurmountable poverty to mental illness and physical ailments. We've accepted an unjust system that thrusts people through to meet arbitrary administrative requirements, resulting in a lack of trust both from people who violate the law and from those who obey it. Ultimately, the system fails everyone.

***

I drink deeply from a well that I did not dig.
DEUTERONOMY 6:11 (KING JAMES VERSION)

I have walked paths that were paved and prepared for me by people who did not even know I was coming. My ancestors constructed, built, mopped, polished, and maintained institutions where I was educated and trained and that they were not permitted to attend. The fact that my ancestors picked cotton and cut sugarcane is not wasted on me. So I serve to pay it back and forward.

I am the daughter of an African American garbageman who was born at Harlem Hospital in New York City in the 1940s. Although he hailed from a progressive city, after the Harlem Renaissance, my father, Allan, spent his summers visiting family in North Carolina, which was under the oppressive grip of Jim Crow laws. There, he experienced racial segregation because of his color and witnessed the violent and deadly legacy of the Ku Klux Klan. He carried the memories of those experiences for a lifetime. By the time my father turned nineteen, President Johnson had signed the Civil Rights Act of 1964, to provide Black people like my dad with the full rights of citizenship. My father never felt that he received them.

Like many African Americans of her generation, my paternal grandmother migrated north. She came from Southern Pines, North Carolina, arriving on the Greyhound bus in New York City in the 1940s. Pregnant with my father, her first child, she moved into the Harlem tenements on Lennox

Avenue. My father was born a Negro, transitioned to Black and proud, and ultimately died an African American. All those attempts at self-determination and self-realization never loosened the chokehold of racism that permeated and traumatized his life.

I am also the daughter of a Dominican beautician who came to this country for a better life for her future children. Now that's visionary, planning for the children who haven't yet arrived. Her goals and intentions were identical to those embraced by the people being held at our borders today in modern-day incarceration camps, separated from their children.

Born under the tyrannical regime of dictator Rafael Trujillo, who ruled the Dominican Republic from 1930 to 1961, my mother, Elsa, grew up in poverty and lived in fear. She was extremely bright, courageous, determined, and resourceful. Armed with an eighth-grade education, she set out for the United States to realize its promises and to make a contribution of her own. She obtained her GED while raising her children. With her limited proficiency in English, she knew that education was the greatest equalizer to pull people out of poverty. Therefore, she made sure her children obtained the best education she could afford for them. However, the lessons she taught her son and daughter about humanity, respect, charity, and love were what were truly invaluable.

My mother was the first humanitarian I ever met and remains the most noble. In the city that helped raise me, Newark, New Jersey, she worked as a beautician for over twenty-five years. A beautiful Afro-Latina with coffee-colored skin, Ms. Elsa, as she was lovingly known, had almond-shaped eyes, pronounced cheekbones, and a magical smile that made her a knockout. I often spent my Saturdays at the salon running from one beauty-supply store to another picking up products for her. I also spent my time listening to the African American, Latina, and immigrant women talk about and reflect on their lives. Ms. Elsa didn't have to articulate her beliefs in proverbs or metaphors. Her actions demonstrated that she didn't believe that marginalized people deserved our scorn; rather, they deserved compassion. She taught my brother, Allen Jr. (officials at the hospital spelled his name differently from how our father's was spelled), and me that even the most vulnerable among us had an untold story. She believed that people's stories contributed to their behavior or their circumstances. Her actions also taught the individuals around her how to treat others with patience, kindness, and understanding. My mother used her life as a force for good. Filled with purpose, she was a fountain of love and compassion.

Ms. Elsa's beauty salon was down the street from the courthouse in Newark, where I would later serve as the chief judge. She was an anchor in that neighborhood and in the local business community. I watched her engage the homeless, whom she fed, and the drug-addicted and despondent, whom she counseled. In her broken English, she communicated with a serene voice and an open heart. As a young person, I never fully understood what drew her to these perplexing people. But mostly I didn't understand what drew them to her. I later understood that they realized that she saw them beyond their brokenness.

I remember that she could walk outside and, from the stoop of her salon, deal with two grown men engaged in a fistfight by yelling, "You know you no supposed to be doing this!"

Embarrassed, the men would stop dead in their tracks, separate, and contritely respond, "You right, Ma. You right. Sorry, sorry."

When her car would not start, her homeless neighbors would wait with her into the night until someone came to pick her up. Or they'd stand with her at the bus stop to ensure her safety. The neighborhood burglar (everyone knew who he was) would chip away at a store's padlock for hours. He would hope to break into a shop to find money or items to sell to buy drugs. My mom never had a metal gate over the glass windowpane that encased her salon's entrance. All the burglar needed to do was throw a rock, and he could get into Ms. Elsa's shop and clean her out. However, not even in his drug-induced state did he rob my mother's business. The neighborhood had a moral code when it came to Ms. Elsa: they would not violate their relationship with her. Not because of fear, not because of her position, and not because of money. They were responding to love. She had become a legitimate authority among the people in the community through the way she treated them, communicated with them, cared for them, and respected them.

She directed longtime customers who had lost their jobs to continue to show up for their appointments. "You come anyway. You pay me when you get new job. But if you no feel good about you hair, you no feel good about you, and you no can get a new job like that," my mother would say.

She used hair care to peek into people's souls and help them heal. She would leave a hard day's work and visit HIV patients in the hospital. During the 1980s, many families discarded HIV-positive relatives because of their health status, but Ms. Elsa was there to help those patients through the challenging times.

My mother's ability to see a person's humanity was so pronounced that I could not help but be deeply influenced by it. Not to mention that she drummed those values into her children. Through her example, a sense of moral obligation to see people holistically by taking everything into consideration seeped into my consciousness, becoming a part of how I administered justice. Naturally, I carried those values into the courtroom setting. This is why I am so passionate about fairness and respect.

One event crystallizes how my mom's philosophical approach has influenced my practice of procedural justice and fairness. I arrived at the beauty parlor after a law school class and found Tyrone, one of the more annoying homeless adults she looked after, sitting in the reception area, his belongings spread out. Agitated, I advised my mother that she couldn't have this person in there with her paying customers. She quickly admonished me in Spanish, which always carried a greater sting. "You treat everyone as if they are a child of God," she said. "And he is sitting there because I said he could."

"Yes, ma'am," I replied, remembering my place.

Ms. Elsa's compassion created a safe space for those in need. She became concerned after one of her clients, Catherine, missed some appointments. Catherine's son had recently been killed, and she was not working. When my mom had seen her the last time, she noticed that Catherine didn't quite seem like herself, acting a little sluggish and forgetful. Since Catherine lived by herself and had lost her income, my mom began to worry. My mother decided to call Catherine and tell her to take a cab, which my mom paid for, to come to the salon and get her hair done. My mom bought her breakfast and lunch. Later she called a cab to take Catherine home. She was worried about the effects of Catherine's prolonged isolation, so she decided to do something about it, letting her spend time at the beauty shop even when she didn't have money. My mother treated her as if she were a neighbor, not a nuisance. Ms. Elsa's beauty salon was open and welcoming to all.

I began to engage in a similar practice in court, without deliberately modeling my mother. I hoped that marginalized people would come to see the courtroom as a place that cared for them. Often the mentally ill and the homeless who came to court would stay for the entire session. I would ask the officers to give them a spare breakfast or lunch out of the stash of extras they usually kept on hand for people in custody. People who are continually hungry don't function well and are usually unco-operative. Some would come early for their clinic appointments and wait in the courtroom. Others without appointments came to see what services might be available to them, and I'd have a caseworker talk to them, possibly connecting them to resources. Sometimes the caseworker would simply guide them to a center where they could take a shower or do a free load of laundry. Our staff would help the poor, homeless, and mentally ill in the neighborhood get their basic human needs met. On some days, former defendants would walk into the courtroom without be-ing summoned and merely sit. When a defendant completed their mandate, I always ended by instructing them, "Come back and let me know how you are doing." They would oblige.

I realized I was channeling Ms. Elsa when Ms. Banks, a homeless woman with schizophrenia, came to court while having a psychotic episode. She was practically yelling at the voices in her head. Some audience members snickered; oth-ers laughed aloud, watching her animated chatter. I looked up from writing on the face of a file. There was no way I was going to allow the snickering and laughing to go unaddressed. The courtroom needed to be a safe place for everyone.

After I addressed her case and Ms. Banks stepped out of the courtroom, I admonished the wrongdoers in the room with a raised eyebrow:

Some of you saw Ms. Banks's condition and thought it was funny. Instead of laughing, you should've been grateful that you haven't reached your threshold. We all have one. It's that event that when it happens, your mind says, "This is too much to bear," and it shuts down. That event could be the loss of a child, the loss of a parent, the loss of a job, illness, or even an injury. The event is so overwhelming, your mind just clocks out, or it turns on itself. So if you could laugh at her, you just haven't met your threshold, and I hope you don't. Instead of laughing, you should be looking at her with compassion and gratitude. You never know. You might be next. So instead of it being a time for laughter, let's make it a time for compassion for someone like Ms. Banks.

My courtroom, my rules.

My mom believed that people should be treated respectfully, no matter their status or circumstances. It always amazed me how effortless it was for her to live these ideals. She combined humility with a strong sense of herself when engaging everyone. This combination ensured she wouldn't get seduced by class, titles, or the trappings of others' success. She respected people, and she didn't see herself as any more or any less than anyone else. She believed that treating everyone respectfully didn't take anything from you or make you appear weak. She always had an extra plate of food, and her home always had a space for people to stay. She mastered the art of the uncomfortable-but-necessary conversation. My philosophy as a judge reflects my mom's philosophy of life.

Ms. Elsa's lessons served her even at the end of her life. On June 2, 2021 (while I was writing this book), after she had endured a long battle with dementia and spent three weeks on life support fighting sepsis, my brother and I, with great heartache, decided to take our beloved mother off the ventilator so she could gracefully move on. Fortunately, she passed as peacefully as she had lived.

As I was making funeral arrangements, I met with the funeral director and the assistant mortician, Ms. Beverly. The funeral director told me that she had been surprised to learn that I, her new client, was in fact Judge Pratt, a "highly respected judge doing God's work." She looked at the assistant mortician and then turned to me and said, "Ms. Beverly would like to thank you."

I was confused. Ms. Beverly had been preparing my mother's body for the funeral, and if anything I should have been thanking her. She had been incredibly helpful and kind during such a difficult time. I looked at her quizzically. Ms. Beverly removed her mask to reveal her face and said, "I wanna thank you, because after I sat in your court all day, you got rid of all of my fines because I was doing well on probation."

The funeral director continued, "And because you got rid of her fines, she was able to go to school and get her license to become a mortician."

I was shocked and at a loss for words. I had no idea that Ms. Beverly and I had had a previous encounter in my court. I said, "Why would I want to keep you bound by a financial yoke when you were doing what the system required?"

How could I have known that my habit of practicing my mother's lesson of treating people with dignity and respect would result in my mother's being treated with the same care by a mortician after her death? Ms. Beverly's kind treatment extended not just to my family, but to all the Essex County families in grief, especially during the COVID-19 pandemic. When she had been caught up in the justice system, she had complied with every aspect of her probation, except the untenable part, the fees imposed by the court. That financial obligation was a hindrance to the very thing the justice system required: for her to become a contributing member of society. In her role as an assistant mortician, Ms. Beverly had patiently listened as I told stories of my mother's unflinching love, kindness, and generosity. She sympathized with me when I said I thought I would be mentally and emotionally prepared for my mother's death, but I wasn't.

Ms. Beverly has been restored to make significant contributions to society. In her story, Ms. Elsa's example once again confirmed for me that people deserve opportunities to be the best selves they can become. Acts of grace are acts of fairness that can have enormous effects on the receiver's life.

***

My perspective on procedural justice has also been shaped in other ways. Since my graduation from law school, I have worked in various capacities throughout the state. Among other positions, I served in Trenton, the state's capital, as assistant counsel in the authorities unit in the governor's counsel's office, and as the compliance officer for the Camden City School District.

I also worked on campaigns supporting progressive candidates. The most valuable part of going door to door, promoting candidates, and describing their platforms was talking to the residents. From the frontlines, I heard their concerns and observed their culturally and often racially varied communities. This experience made me conversant in how the individuals, residential homes, public housing complexes, businesses, houses of worship, schools, and parks coalesced to form neighborhoods. In turn, the neighborhoods created distinctive wards that pieced together the city. Learning to listen to others helped me keep my finger on the pulse of things.

Later in my career, a few significant encounters informed my drive for reform. One day, as I waited for my training session as a brand-new judge, the veteran judge flew into the chambers, running incredibly late. He exchanged his overcoat and suit jacket for a robe and gave me a quick spiel about his court. The court staff announced us, we entered the courtroom, and I sat in the chair next to him on the bench. And then speed court began.

I've done speed dating, but this went even faster. There were quick exchanges between the judge, the attorneys, and the staff. The judge rapidly marked documents and files with a metal stamp that sounded like a cash register. It left tiny, illegible words blemished with heavy ink splotches. The judge placed check marks in what appeared to be arbitrary boxes and scribbled his signature. After half an hour of observing this, my head was reeling. If I didn't know what was happening when I was sitting next to him, what were the defendants experiencing? He then hopped off the bench to complete probable cause and set bails on arrest warrants. He quizzed me on setting bails. He was moving so quickly that I continued to struggle to understand.

At one point, he was making a bail determination on an eighteen-year-old arrested for distribution and possession who had one prior conviction. He wanted to test my judgment, so he asked for my recommendation. Referencing my handy bail guidelines, I said it called for a minimum of $25,000 with a 10 percent option. This meant the young man would need to post $2,500 to be released.

As the judge continued to stamp and sign swiftly, he said, "No. I'm going to give him $50,000 in cash or bond because I need to teach him a lesson."

It struck me in the gut that the judge was setting an improper bail simply for pedagogic purposes. The amount of bail he imposed greatly exceeded the guidelines for what the charge should have been. More precisely, he was giving the young man an excessive bail to feed his own ego. Or maybe he was exacting some form of revenge for a time when he felt bullied by tough guys in his youth. Whatever it was, it was not justice.

I have thought about that experience often. If the proceedings left me dizzy, confused, and frustrated, how did laypeople understand them? They didn't. And whether they understood the process or not didn't seem to matter.

I did, however, appreciate learning what *not* to do. Largely, the experience reminded me to question—and check—my ego constantly.

***

There's a lyric repeated in a few songs that says when you die, your headstone will have two dates on it, but the only thing that matters is the line in between. Every day when I wake up, I lie about the first date—a women's birthright—and I try to extend the last date. This book is about the line in between: my lifelong work to improve justice, guarantee fairness, and ensure just outcomes for everyone.

Here, I tell the story of reforming my court and impacting the lives of those who came through that court and those who worked there. I chronicle what amazed me, distressed me, infuriated me, made me laugh, and ultimately enlightened me.

Life does some mean, nasty things to people that can drop them to their knees. Life then stands over them and dares them to stand up. Most people don't. They stay in that low place, make it their station in life, and gauge their entire existence from there. They decide what they can or cannot do and who they can or cannot become based on that position. And then they experience a contact with the criminal justice system that has disastrous consequences.

One day, a defendant said, "I've got to stand on my own ten."

"What does that mean, young man?" I asked.

"It means I have to learn how to stand on my own feet, Judge," he explained.

I hope this book will help people stand on their own and not shrink from their responsibility to address injustice wherever they see it, especially when they are a part of the system creating the injustice. My wish is that this radically human approach to justice changes how we live in our countries, states, and neighborhoods. And beyond that, my hope is that the stories presented here will be lessons that people can apply when engaging others in any industry, organization, business, or relationship. When everyone is treated with dignity, the possibilities for all our communities are truly limitless.

Chapter 1

A BETTER APPROACH

A nation's success or failure in achieving democracy is judged in part by how well it responds to those at the bottom and the margins of the social order.
—SANDRA DAY O'CONNOR

Picture this. Newark Municipal Court, in Newark, New Jersey, summer of 2012. It felt as hot as the sun itself in the Brick City, Newark's moniker. Of course, the faithful air conditioner was out of commission in courtroom 222, which housed Part Two Criminal Court, unaffectionately known as "the Deuce." A sea of Black and Brown faces—mostly Black and belonging to mostly poor and mostly marginalized people—packed the Deuce. It was your typical urban courtroom, inundated by low-level offenders with high-level problems. For them, seemingly insignificant interactions with the justice system upend their lives.

My tiny desk fan was rattling. Beads of sweat gathered between my shoulder blades and inched down my back as I worked feverishly in my black robe, made of my girls Poly and

Ester. It was one of those days when the more people I moved out of the courtroom, the more people seemed to pop up in their place.

Jamal Hinner, a solidly built young African American man with a honey brown complexion in a striped, short-sleeve polo shirt and jeans, walked into the courtroom and plopped himself down on a rear bench. I hadn't seen him in years. I felt my irritation rise while he sat there with a blank stare, his mouth slightly agape. *Why is he here, again?* I wondered as I gave him the side-eye.

He was about twenty-two years old, but he had started getting arrested and appearing before me at age eighteen. Initially, I found his cases a bit odd. They were all harassment cases brought by his family members. He would go to his relatives' homes and incessantly ring the doorbell. Or he would stand outside their houses and yell at their windows. Instead of letting him in, they called the police. I later learned that the early signs of schizophrenia began to reveal themselves in males at around eighteen years of age.

After we successfully got him through Newark Community Solutions—a court program that provides alternative sentencing—he returned to my courtroom on new charges. When I called the next case, I noticed that he had put his headphones on and was rocking in his seat.

I said sternly, "Mr. Hinner, you know you can't listen to music in court. Take your headphones off." I shook my head in disapproval as a bead of sweat gathered at my right temple.

He rolled his eyes as he removed his earphones. I quickly realized that this exchange was about my own misunderstanding. What was he doing? He was drowning out the voices in his head. He suffered from auditory hallucinations, which cause a person to hear voices or music without any external stimulation. He attempted to cope with his condition by playing music louder than he hoped the voices could speak. Unfortunately, I missed it.

I knew about his diagnosis, but in the heat I had forgotten to consider what it took for him to make it through a day in court. Watching Mr. Hinner out of the corner of my eye, I noticed that the forty-something-year-old white police officer assigned to my court had walked past him and stopped as if rooted to the spot. The young man must've muttered something. The officer did a double take and furrowed his eyebrows. Officer Albert Cosgrove—an athletic, dark-haired, twenty-year police veteran—looked over his shoulder and responded to Mr. Hinner's comment. Then he shook his head and kept walking.

I wondered, *Why is Officer Cosgrove talking to Mr. Hinner? Doesn't he remember that Mr. Hinner's schizophrenia makes him hate and act aggressively toward police officers?*

Then it hit me like a high-speed moving train. Damn. The police officers assigned to my court that day had been working with me for less than a year; they didn't know Mr. Hinner, and Mr. Hinner didn't know them. While the officers weren't new to the police force, they were new to my courtroom and certain defendants. In this case they had no experience with Mr. Hinner, one of the more challenging defendants who ended up in my courtroom.

"Mr. Hinner! Mr. Hinner!" I yelled as I signaled with a hand gesture for him to approach counsel's table. "Your case is next. Come up, come up, come up!"

Officer Marion Solomon, an older, husky, paternal African American man, casually walked over to Mr. Hinner and tapped him on the shoulder. "Son," he said, "the judge just called your case."

Oh, no, I thought, squeezing my eyes shut. *Officer Solomon touched him*. My chest tightened.

Even though no single wave is responsible for a tsunami, I could not shirk from responsibility for the mayhem that was about to ensue. I pride myself on giving people who work in my court a heads-up about challenging defendants. On this day, a massive caseload, my irritation with Mr. Hinner, and my preoccupation with moving cases along caused me to forget to attend to that detail.

It all happened so quickly. Mr. Hinner shot out of his seat like a rocket. He landed with his chest out, his finger pointed in Officer Solomon's face, and yelling profanities. Before I knew it, the two police officers and the court attendant were restraining Mr. Hinner, who was lifting three-hundred-pound Officer Solomon off the ground. Officer Cosgrove had Mr. Hinner in a chokehold. He was no longer restraining Mr. Hinner. He was in a fight.

I had no instruction manual on how to handle the situation that was unfolding before me. Like other judges, I had only received guidance suggesting that when an incident occurs in your courtroom, get off the bench for your own safety and avoid becoming a witness to the situation. But I believe that my job is to serve as a leader in that courtroom, not to run and hide when an incident occurs. I was not going to abandon ship. For Mr. Hinner, because of his decompensating mental state, the mere touch of the officer had felt like an assault. The police officers were responding according to their training, not with some malice of heart or desire to unleash violence on the young man.

As I watched the chaos—audience members running for cover, staffers leaving their posts, everyone observing in horror—all I could think of was Eric Garner. Mr. Garner, an unarmed African American man, was killed by a New York City police officer who placed him in a chokehold after stopping him for selling cigarettes. As the pandemonium ensued in my courtroom, it was like I experienced déjà vu. Vivid images of news footage flashed through my mind of Mr. Garner lying on the ground in a chokehold, gasping for air, being restrained by officers as he repeatedly cried out, "I can't breathe." This phrase, this plea for mercy, became the rallying cry for protesters across the country. I said to myself, *Not here. Not today.*

According to the research, individuals with untreated mental illness, like Mr. Hinner, are sixteen times more likely to be killed during encounters with law enforcement than those who are mentally sound.[1] Those killed by police are also disproportionately Black and Native American.[2] Imagine the number of mentally ill people who have nonfatal yet traumatizing encounters with the police because of their mental state. This abuse continues throughout their contact with the justice system—in the courts, probation, jail or prison, and parole. This is because justice system actors expect people to comply with their rules and obey commands upon issuance. They don't concern themselves with a person's limitations and how those limitations make it temporarily—or often permanently—impossible for the person to accomplish the task. Commands as trivial as "Sit quietly in court," "Stop making so much noise on this corner," "Show up to your probation check-in on July 3" are not easily accomplished when you suffer from auditory hallucinations.

This is compounded by the stark differences in perceptions of fairness in our country. According to a Pew Research Center study, 68 percent of Black people surveyed said that Black people are generally treated less fairly by the court system than

whites, while only 27 percent of white people surveyed believe
that Blacks are treated unfairly by the justice system.[3] Rekia
Boyd, Michael Brown, George Floyd, Eric Garner, Daunte
Wright, Breonna Taylor, and Lewis Sanks King . . . police
shootings and killings of unarmed Black men and women
seem never-ending. This unequal treatment extends to the imposition of harsh and disparate sentences for the same crimes.
People of color, historically and presently, have faced injustice
from the criminal justice system. And they carry memories
of their own experiences and those of their friends, families,
neighbors, and acquaintances when they attend court to respond to their cases.

Even without an instructional manual, I had spent invaluable years watching Ms. Elsa, my mom, handle the drug-
addicted, the mentally ill, and the emotionally unstable at her
beauty salon. Borrowing from Ms. Elsa's playbook, I sat forward in my seat, lowered my voice, and said, "Mr. Hinner,
it's Judge Pratt. Please, listen to my voice. The police officers
are not trying to hurt you. I need you to stop moving." At the
same time, I gently gestured with my hands for him to stop.

While trying to break free, he responded, "Tell them to get
off of me, Judge!"

"Cosgrove, release his neck," I said. Officer Cosgrove gave
me an incredulous look, as if I had lost my entire mind. Nowhere in his twenty years on the police force had he been
trained to respond in the way I was directing. However, he had
previously told me that he had seen things happen in my courtroom that he'd never seen in the course of his career. He knew
that I had a way of handling challenging people and difficult
situations that brought about what he viewed as unbelievably

positive outcomes. He trusted me, so he released the young man from the chokehold.

Huffing and puffing, Officer Solomon and the court attendant both followed suit and released Mr. Hinner.

I told Mr. Hinner to wait outside the courtroom, and I directed the court administrator to give him a new court date. Mr. Hinner was willing to listen to me because he had spent time in my courtroom, where he had been treated with kindness, acceptance, and respect. He trusted that I would keep the officers from hurting him. In my courtroom, everyone responded to his condition in a respectful, patient manner that allowed him to maintain his dignity.

Officer Cosgrove approached the bench and said, "He'll be worse when he comes back, Judge."

I replied, "Watch." Procedural justice, and the other techniques I used to build trust, saved the day—and a life—on that sweltering morning in the Deuce.

Two weeks passed, and Mr. Hinner returned to court. When I called his case, I told him, "Young man, you owe this court an apology."

Officer Cosgrove ran to the front of the courtroom and interrupted me. "Judge, we worked it out. It was all a misunderstanding." He shook Mr. Hinner's hand. Wow.

Mr. Hinner was readmitted to the program. A while later, he walked into court on a random day. "Mr. Hinner, you don't have court today," I said.

"I'm not here to see you, Judge," he sharply responded, as if I had taken liberty with my assumption that a person coming to court might be there to see me. He walked over to Officer Cosgrove, who dug into his wallet to give Mr. Hinner lunch money to buy a soda and a hot dog from the cart in front of the courthouse. This became a regular occurrence. Or Officer Solomon would give him an extra lunch from those they had brought to the cellblock for people being detained. At one point, after Mr. Hinner had been detained and sent to the county jail due to a probation violation on a superior court matter, Officer Solomon called the sheriff's officers to advise them on how to handle him.

It was sad to witness Mr. Hinner's mental health drive his contacts with the criminal justice system. And even the justice system's well-intentioned attempts to address his behavior, like placing him on probation, were woefully inadequate. As it exists in our county, the probation system requires one officer to supervise between 100 and 125 probationers. That is a system designed to fail. Then, at a hearing to address a violation of probation, the court is asked to sort it out by reinstating this unsuccessful relationship or sending the violator to jail.

Although serious issues exist in the court system for addressing people with mental health needs, I still managed to find ways to turn my courtroom into a resource. The feelings of trust and mutual respect I established created an environment where veteran police officers and a young African American man with schizophrenia were willing to step outside the heat of the moment during one eventful day and behave in an unprecedented way. There was no arrest and no trip to the coroner's office. Mr. Hinner realized that these uniformed officers were not trying to hurt him. The officers became better at crisis intervention and at recognizing that many factors could be motivating a person's behavior.

***

Every day across America, people walk into our courts entering a world that is foreign, intimidating, and often quite hostile to them. They are routinely confused by the nature of their charges and annoyed about their encounters with police. Participants can find the process of attending court humiliating. They are standing in front of strangers, addressing their legal matters, while the audience hears the worst aspects of their life. They are afraid they will not have a compassionate, open-minded judge hearing their case. Many court participants fear that the judge might see them as just another Black or Brown face in crisis. If the judge appears to dislike them before even hearing their story, how can they believe the process is fair?

Let me walk you through what it is like for an average person that comes through our courthouses. First, they encounter a person in the lobby wearing a bulletproof vest and herding them through security. Guards shout for them to remove clothing and discard personal items: "Take off your belts, pull out your keys, throw out your lighters."

After being prodded through security, they eventually stumble into the building. Then they walk around and ask different people, who appear to be court employees, the same question—"How do I find the courtroom I'm supposed to be in?"—and receive different answers. When they finally get to the right courtroom, they encounter another person in an official uniform chastising them for violating rules they didn't know existed. "Take off your hat! Pull up your pants! Tuck in your shirt! Take your arms off the back of the bench! No reading in court!" They check in with the court attendant and find and settle into a seat. Their attorney flies into court at the last moment and essentially tells them to shut up because the attorney has everything under control. When the judge finally gets on the bench, then it really gets bad.

What if I told you that you could improve people's court experience, increase the public's trust in the justice system, increase compliance with court orders, and reduce crime with a simple idea? Well, that simple idea is procedural justice, also known as procedural fairness.

It's a concept that says if people perceive that the individuals in authority in the justice system are treating them fairly, and with dignity and respect, they will obey the law. That's what Tom Tyler, a Yale psychologist, found when he began to study procedural justice back in the 1970s. He found that if people began to see the actors in the justice system as legitimate authorities for setting rules and regulations, they would follow those rules.[4] In his book *David and Goliath*, Malcolm Gladwell writes, "Legitimacy is based on three things. First of all, the people who are asked to obey authority have to feel like they have a voice—that if they speak up, they will be heard. Second, the law has to be predictable. There has to be a reasonable expectation that the rules tomorrow are going to be roughly the same as the rules today. And third, the authority has to be fair. It can't treat one group differently from another."[5]

People will allow themselves to be subject to a governing body's authority if they know the authority will listen to them. People must also be able to anticipate legal outcomes. And the governing body must be fair. This notion further supports Tom Tyler's research, which concluded that if people believed they were treated with dignity and respect, and fairly, they would be willing to accept the judge's rulings, even when the judge ruled against them. His research demonstrated that procedural justice was essential in transforming the court's relationship with the community.[6]

Procedural justice is different from distributive justice, which is solely concerned with outcomes: winning or losing a case. It is not that people don't want to win their cases. Rather, the interpersonal interactions they have with the justice system guide their determinations as to whether the process was fair. And the most significant determining factor in whether a person feels the process was procedurally just is the judge. This perception of fairness is shaped by how the judge speaks to court participants. The good news is that the principles of procedural fairness are simple and can be implemented in any system as quickly as tomorrow. Even better, they can be implemented for free.

In their article "Procedural Justice from the Bench: How Judges Can Improve the Effectiveness of Criminal Courts," Greg Berman and Emily Gold discuss data from a study undertaken by the Urban Institute, the Center for Court Innovation, and the Research Triangle Institute that supports this proposition.[7] The evaluation compared defendants in twenty-three drug courts with those in six traditional criminal courts. In traditional courts, drug-addicted defendants convicted of drug offenses are punished with severe, extended periods of incarceration in an approach that focuses on punishment and uses prison sentences as a deterrent for future criminal behavior.

In contrast, drug court programs provide an alternative to incarceration by acknowledging that drug addiction is a disease and that incarceration is not a cure, nor does it provide the behavior modification the court seeks. As a result, drug court judges focus on drug treatment and on motivating defendants through positive reinforcement so they successfully complete the treatment and improve their lives. The foundation of their approach is procedural justice.

In traditional courts, by contrast, the judge is generally focused on calendar management, guilt and innocence, and how much punishment is necessary. There are no, or few, inquiries into the underlying cause of the defendant's actions. Problem-solving courts, such as drug courts, focus on addressing social ills. The traditional court's emphasis on case management—how quickly the case can be moved through the system—leaves very little time for communication and consideration.

The study described in Berman and Gold's article documented that drug courts are successful in helping participants achieve sobriety. Participants were substantially less likely to report drug use eighteen months after admission to the program. Even those who continued using drugs did so less regularly than those in the traditional court system. Drug court participants also reported engaging in considerably fewer illegal acts than the traditional group, reducing their unlawful activity by over 50 percent. The drug courts in the study saved money: over $5,600 per participant.

The study showed impressive results for courts that worked with high-level offenders, revealing that the courts weren't successful simply because they were drug courts. The data demonstrated that the defendant's positive attitude toward the judge was the most critical factor in determining future criminal behavior. Defendants with positive perceptions of the judge had less drug use, committed fewer supervision violations, and reported less illicit behavior. The positive perceptions resulted because they perceived that the judge treated them fairly.

For me, being a judge is like having a reserved seat to a tragic reality show with no commercial interruptions and never-ending seasons of trauma. At one point, I realized that court participants' need for help was greater than my fear of appearing vulnerable on the bench. I realized that not only did I need to do something, but I could, in fact, do something.

In all honesty, I knew nothing about procedural justice when I got on the bench. One day, Greg Berman, then the executive director of the Center for Court Innovation (and one of the authors of the article described above), came to observe my court with his staff. Afterward, I got off the bench to greet them in my chambers, as I did with all visitors. Mr. Berman gave me a look that was both puzzled and pleased. He said, "Does that just come naturally to you?"

Slightly embarrassed, I tilted my head and gave him a nervous smile. I appeared to be the only one in the room who didn't know what initiated that question. He continued his inquisition, asking, "Have you heard of procedural justice?" I hadn't.

"There is a theory out there that talks about everything you're doing in your court," Mr. Berman said. I raised my eyebrow because I didn't understand what those things were.

I subsequently read Tom Tyler's book, *Why People Obey the Law*, and learned about the data that supported principles I knew anecdotally and had applied intuitively. Good judges across the country were engaging in practices that had transformational effects on the people they served. No, I'm not deluded by the idea of easy solutions. Yes, the court has limitations as it responds to the cases before it. Judges don't control the promulgation of laws. That is a function of the legislative branch. Judges don't control the first point of contact. That is the role of law enforcement. But I propose that the work of procedural justice can begin when people step foot in the courtroom. An anonymous quote says, "Law: The only place where the best players get to sit on the bench." And with that privilege comes the obligation, the responsibility, for judges to do better.

Several principles underlie the practice of procedural justice. The rest of the chapter examines them and shows them in practice.

Voice

Giving people an opportunity to tell their side of the story is crucial when building the public's trust in the justice system. Even when you are not going to let them speak, you must explain why: "Procedurally, sir, it's not time to take your testimony. I'll hear what you want to share at the next court date." "Ma'am, you are not represented by counsel right now, so I'm not going to let you say anything that might hurt your case. The prosecutor is listening and may use your statement against you." I say we should allow people to speak during the court process, knowing that many courts are busy places that cannot afford to let everyone engage in unlimited conversations. I am not suggesting we permit individuals to give Shakespearean monologues. But listening does allow for more just outcomes. The investment of giving defendants voice on the front end is well worth the rewards on the back end. As a side note, this may have some limitations with defendants in higher-level cases where there are serious concerns about self-incrimination.

For me, the assignment of essays was instrumental in giving people voice. Not only did they have to write the essays, but they also had to read them in open court. Making them read aloud in court increased the quality of what they shared. I assigned topics such as "If I Believed One Positive Thing About Myself, How Would My Life Be Different?," "Letter to My Teenage Self," "Letter to My Son or Daughter," "If I Knew Then What I Know Now, How Would My Life Be Different?" Contemplating these issues was often cathartic for the writers. It also forced them to unearth and address the pain that ultimately caused them to appear in court. I sometimes required young men to read and write a reaction to a *New York Times* editorial board op-ed titled "Forcing Black Men Out of Society," and women to read and react to chapters from *Misguided Justice: The War on Drugs and the Incarceration of Black Women*, by Stephanie R. Bush-Baskette.[8]

I once assigned an essay to a first-year, eighteen-year-old college student. He was one of almost twenty-five students who had received summonses in ongoing raids on college parties by the university's police force. He looked like a young Jason Bateman, with a cowlick emerging from his dark hair. Dressed in a preppy polo shirt and jeans, he always sat close to his friend toward the back of the courtroom. As he stood before me reading his essay, he lamented his summons, which was for underage drinking. He said his roommate told him not to go to the party, but he had wanted to fit in. He said he worried he would become an alcoholic like his mom, who had died a few months prior as a result of liver disease.

Writing an essay provides opportunities for both defendant and judge. The defendant has a chance to reflect. The judge gets information beyond the charges and criminal record before them, which helps them make a more informed decision. It allows the judge to see more than the one moment in time that brings a person to court. It forces them to see the whole person and the larger story, beyond a mere incident or single crime. We typically only hear personal information about the defendant at sentencing, when it is delivered to help mitigate their sentence, to lessen their time in traditional court. Imagine starting with that information earlier, as you craft an appropriate punishment. Imagine using the personal information that keeps the individual entangled in a life of crime to create a plan that helps them deal with trauma and overcome social and personal pressures. That is why the essays are instrumental. They are honest, cathartic, and revealing. Traditional courts receive this critical information far too late in the process, leaving the judge with an incomplete picture.

Essays counteract the narrow scope in which defendants are permitted to speak in court, if they speak at all. Their attorneys often advise them to keep their remarks to a minimum. When they do speak, they are required to contort their story into courtroom-speak.

Neutrality

In working to increase the public trust in the justice system, neutrality is paramount. It is intrinsically connected to fairness. If the public does not believe in the process by which people in authority arrive at their decisions, whether to stop, indict, or convict, then there can be no trust in the system. The judge cannot be perceived as being partial to one side over the other. The judge has to make a conscious decision to avoid saying things like "my officer," "my prosecutor," "my defense attorney." And this is challenging. People are assigned to a particular court, so judges see the same attorneys practicing before them day in and day out.

It becomes incredibly challenging to preserve the appearance of neutrality when legal processes that occur in the middle of proceedings—like sidebars and conferencing cases in chambers—erode that appearance. A sidebar is a discussion between the judge and counsel outside the earshot of the jury, the audience, and usually the actual parties to the proceedings. This process gets especially tricky when the defendant is self-represented. In those instances, judges rarely call them up to discuss issues in the case due to safety concerns. Conferencing a case is another off-the-record discussion that usually happens in the judge's chambers, leaving interested or observing parties wondering about the secretive meeting. What are they discussing? What information is the judge considering? Why can't we hear?

When I think of neutrality, I'm reminded of being a new Rutgers Law grad and freshly minted attorney. Early in my career, I went to work for an insurance-defense law firm. The new law associates were usually sent down to the "cattle call," or arbitration hearings. These mandatory hearings were a way to resolve disputes before a case could proceed to trial. Other attorneys served as the arbitrators. During the hearings, lawyers provided documentation and presented or refuted the facts, depending on which party they represented. After hearing both sides, the impartial and neutral arbitrator was required to determine a fair monetary award or to find that no award was warranted. After preparing a case for my client one morning, I waited to have my case called.

•

When it was called, I nervously gathered my files and proceeded to find the assigned room. Since I was new to this, it took me a minute to get my bearings and locate the hearing room. When I finally arrived, I encountered two gray-haired gentlemen—my adversary, who was representing the plaintiff, and the arbitrator—in the middle of an overly friendly conversation. Their tone with one another was relaxed and familiar. They finally greeted me and returned to their chummy conversation. As I got settled at the table, I realized they were so friendly with each other because they were friends.

These veterans had been practicing law as colleagues for years. They played golf together and saw each other socially. That morning they were even discussing scheduling their next round of golf. My client couldn't get a fair assessment of the plaintiff's case in this hearing. I didn't ask for a new arbitrator because, based on the years of practice required to become an arbitrator, my adversary probably knew them all. What made the situation feel worse was their lack of discretion about their relationship: they didn't at all attempt to foster the appearance of neutrality. Before we even started arbitration, I knew I would be rejecting the arbitrator's award, requesting a trial de novo, and paying the applicable fee.

It is not uncommon for judges and attorneys to have relationships. Judges at one time were attorneys who worked with, studied with, and even raised their children with other attorneys. Those connections are not easy to ignore. However, there is an obligation to behave with neutrality. In some instances, however, the judiciary responds to relationships that are friendly in a manner that's unreasonable. A recent case provides an example. The New Jersey Supreme Court found that two judges violated ethics rules when they continued to attend church dinners with a group that included a fellow church member who had been indicted on misconduct charges. The Court stated that the judges being seen in public with the indicted church member might be interpreted as a "tacit endorsement" of his innocence.[9] Although the Supreme Court noted that shunning him was not required, their decision required both a social rejection of the other church member and disassociation with a religious group. Must a judge leave the church or move to another pew if an accused person attends the same service? Is a judge prevented from being seen in public with their spouse or child if that person is charged with and subsequently indicted for a crime? Where do we draw the line? This decision creates an untenable situation for judges in their everyday lives. Although the ultimate goal is to promote trust in the judicial system, and to have judges uphold the principle of neutrality, I find this ruling to be extreme.

Understanding

It is critical that people understand the judicial process they are a part of, the consequences of the process, and what is expected of them. I am keenly aware that many of the individuals who appear before me have very little education, they may suffer from mental illness, or English may be their second language. In a typical year, our courthouse provides translators for twenty-four languages. I like to say, "Legalese is the language that we use to confuse." For those reasons, I use plain English in the courtroom. When I was first appointed to the bench, I received a script from a senior judge that included many questions to ask a mentally ill person to determine whether I wanted to request a mental health evaluation. When I saw the first person who I thought suffered from mental illness, I asked the scripted questions. "Sir, do you take, um, psycho—um, psychotropic—psychotropic medication?" I asked. I couldn't even pronounce the word.

He responded, "Nope."

"Sir, have you ever been treated by a psychiatrist?"

"Nope." But it was apparent that he had a mental illness.

In my frustration, one day I decided to scrap the script and ask the defendant one question: "Ma'am, do you take medication to clear your mind?"

She responded, "Yeah, Judge. I take Haldol for my schizophrenia, Xanax for my anxiety. . . ."

The question works even in situations where you think it should not. When confronted with another defendant who appeared to be suffering from mental illness, I asked, "Mr. Lee, do you take medication to clear your mind?"

"No, Judge! I don't take no medication to clear my mind!" he responded gruffly, rolling his eyes at me, as if it were the dumbest question he had heard in his entire life. "I take medication to stop the voices in my head. But my mind is otherwise fine."

"Thank you very much, Mr. Lee. Case dismissed."

The New Jersey Supreme Court has also tasked its judges with identifying veterans who can be linked to services.[10] Unfortunately, many ex-servicemen and -women don't realize they are entitled to benefits and services. Newark Penn Station is considered the state's largest unofficial homeless shelter. Good Samaritans go there daily to provide the homeless with food, and a medical van goes there weekly. Commuters give the homeless at the station money just to get them out of their path. We worked with a nonprofit veterans' organization that conducted interviews from midnight to three a.m. at Newark Penn Station to identify and provide services to homeless veterans. They once encountered a gentleman who had done three tours in Vietnam and had been homeless and staying at Penn Station for ten years. When asked why he hadn't gone to the Department of Veterans Affairs for assistance, he told them that he hadn't gotten hurt during his tours, so he was not a veteran. Within a week, the organization helped him get out of Newark Penn Station and into veterans' housing, and also helped him obtain the benefits he was owed. He didn't understand that he fit the criteria and was absolutely eligible for benefits. In his mind, he had to have a physical injury to be considered a veteran.

We now know that the psychological injuries and trauma suffered by servicemen and -women are as devastating and debilitating as the physical ones. After speaking to several veterans, I decided to modify how I asked them to identify themselves in my court. I asked, "If you have ever been in the service, if you have ever been in the military, or if you have ever worn the uniform, please let me know." I use their language, how they describe themselves and their experience, to help them identify themselves. In recent years, New Jersey's Administrative Office of the Courts has updated the language used in its Veterans Assistance Project to make it easier to understand.

Understanding, however, must go both ways. Judges must understand the community, its language, and the circumstances that drive people into the courts. I'll never forget Veronica Stratford, a woman brought before me out of the lockup who was charged with soliciting prostitution. Standing there defiantly, she wore a teal-green bolero sweater that matched a brown, white, and teal pleated shirt. She pressed down her short, chocolate-brown hair, which blended into her skin tone. The public defender and prosecutor reported that she had rejected a plea offer that would have imposed a high monetary fine for a guilty plea to prostitution. When I looked at the plea deal, I saw that Ms. Stratford had 101 arrests. I was floored. I had never seen a person with so many arrests and convictions. Her public defender requested that I release her without bail, on her own recognizance, but I could not turn a blind eye to the high number of arrests and convictions. I imposed a bail that was in line with her arrests and convictions for nonviolent offenses. The amount of money didn't matter. She couldn't make bail at any amount. When I saw Ms. Stratford on her next court date, via video from the county jail, her public defender explained that, once again, she had rejected the state's offer. Dressed in her orange jumpsuit, she immediately began to explain. "Judge, I know I'm usually out there doing that. But on the day they stopped me, I was going to a doctor's appointment. I *live* on the ho stroll. I *live* there." The court erupted in laughter.

She's referring to herself as a ho? I wondered. Then I got it. The prostitutes live in the neighborhoods where they work. We all knew the streets that were notorious for prostitution. They were low-rent and high-drug-traffic areas. As I write about the women who came before me on prostitution charges, I do not refer to them as sex workers. I believe it's a mischaracterization. "Worker" suggests that they engage in a voluntary act and not the daily survival tactics of their drug-addicted, trauma-filled, subject-to-constant-violence lives. They are not posting ads on a website or working for a high-end escort agency. Yes, the word "prostitute" connotes a negative, denigrating, unsavory image, and that is exactly what their lives are. Calling them sex workers makes us feel comfortable about their circumstances, as if they have jobs. We need to focus on improving their circumstances, not just giving them nicer names.

"Ma'am, I guess the problem for the police is they don't know when it's your day off," I responded. But I believed her. I dismissed her case for the time she had already served. But this conversation did lend itself to my understanding of police operations. An officer explained that prostitutes were easy arrests. They work and live on the prostitution stroll, so officers routinely conduct raids in those areas and bring them in and process them. The constant raids explain why they tend to have a higher number of arrests.

The seminal New Jersey Supreme Court case *State v. Johnson* set forth eight factors for judges to consider when establishing the monetary amount of bail.[11] This case, which predates New Jersey's reform measures that eliminated monetary bail, included considering the defendant's criminal record and prior history of bail. Having an awareness of arrest practices provided me a better understanding of whether the number of arrests for prostitution truly reflected wrongdoing that warranted a monetary bail. While the intentions of bail are to ensure that the defendant returns to court and to reduce the likelihood that they reoffend, it has morphed into a punitive strategy.

Respect

Without respect, none of the other principles of procedural justice can work. Respect can be as simple as saying, "Good morning, sir," or "Good afternoon, ma'am." I once mentioned this at a panel discussion, and a judge came up to me and said, "You call the defendants 'sir' and 'ma'am'?"

I replied, "Well, if I'm discourteous to someone, it says more about me than it does about them."

It's important to look a person in the eye when you are talking to them, and especially when you are sentencing them. I'm thinking of a jurisdiction that will remain unnamed. The judges there are instructed that when they take adverse action against a defendant—for example, impose a bail, deny their motion, sentence them to jail—they should not look that person in the eye. Instead, they should lower their gaze. Now imagine how the person receiving the adverse action feels about the decision and the decision-maker. They are saying to themselves, *The judge did me dirty. They couldn't even look me in the eye.*

I make it a point to say, "How you doing? What's going on with you today?" And I say it not as a greeting, but as an active listener actually interested in the response. Respect is the difference between saying, "Ma'am, are you having difficulty understanding the information in the paperwork?" versus, "You can read and write, can't you?" when you realize there's a literacy issue. And the good thing about respect is that it's contagious. People see you being respectful to other folks, and they impute that respect to themselves.

Showing people respect also instills confidence in the process and the person in authority, as in the case of Rafiq Morrison. The prosecutor of another court transferred his case to my court so he could be considered for the Newark Community Solutions program. Charged with possessing one marijuana cigarette, the young African American college graduate, a native Newarker, shifted in his seat with nervousness. His father had been involved in the criminal justice system, so he had no faith in the process. He agonized over whether he would be admitted into the program, without which he would be unable to become a licensed teacher.

"I sat in your court and watched how you treated everybody," Mr. Morrison said later, recollecting that day. "You spoke to them, you let them speak to you. You didn't take any stuff from anyone, but you were really respectful to folks. It made me think, *My case is in good hands. When she gets my case, she's going to know what to do.*"

My respectful treatment of others made him feel not only that I was competent, but that I would also be fair. It is important to understand that people are judging our fitness, our capacity to make decisions over their lives. I admitted Mr. Morrison to the program, which he completed. He went on to become a full-time teacher at a middle school, where he mentors young African American and Latino boys. "They see me as their big brother, not only as their teacher. We have the same background, and they realize that they can go to college and succeed," he proudly told me.

A research article titled "What Works? The Ten Key Components of Drug Court: Research-Based Practices" sets forth effective methods for reducing recidivism rates in drug courts. One practice in particular is noteworthy for our purposes. Researchers found that when judges spent an increased amount of time with defendants during court hearings—specifically, an average of three minutes or more per defendant—recidivism was reduced by 153 percent more than in courts where judges spent less time.[12]

The results of this article rely on a significant facet of procedural justice: fairness. The results also coincide with the four central pillars of procedural justice (you will see that these greatly overlap with the four principles I've outlined in this chapter):

- Treating people with dignity and respect
- Allowing individuals to have a voice
- Being neutral in decision-making
- Having trustworthy motives

I would add a fifth to their list: understanding.

Although three minutes may not seem long, that time is significant because it increases the judge's influence and leads to more profound interactions. It also aligns with the principles of procedural justice by giving the individual time to have a voice during the proceedings, allowing greater opportunity to provide clarity (understanding) and to give the appearance of neutrality. And most importantly, the individual feels respected. Reducing recidivism rates is just another advantage of procedural justice.

***

It is important to dispel misconceptions around the use of procedural justice in the courtroom. One mistaken belief is that it hinders accountability. Some claim that treating people with dignity and respect leads to judges being perceived as weak. Some believe that procedural justice is somehow lenient, and that defendants will fake penitence and take advantage of judges.

Yes, a judge can find it challenging to hold people accountable when they are working with a population that cycles repeatedly through the criminal justice system. The person in authority must be consistent, clear about expectations, and unyieldingly fair. Fairness in this context means that the person in authority must keep their word. If I promise a benefit for compliance, the person receives it. And if I promise a punishment for noncompliance, they must receive that as well. Traditionally, our system has only offered punishment for noncompliance, whether guidance for compliance is provided or not.

Moreover, the idea that treating people respectfully signals weakness is ludicrous. My community started using the shorthand slogan "Judge Pratt don't play" to describe my courtroom's reputation. This certainly wasn't because I was perceived as weak. I was always clear when someone received a second chance in my court. That second chance came with requirements, which included showing up on time and not reoffending. Defendants who failed to comply with court orders received specific and immediate consequences.

The requirements of the legal process itself can harden practitioners' hearts. It's difficult to be tasked with arresting people who are drug-sick instead of getting them necessary medical treatment. It can be upsetting to address defendants who are clearly suffering from the side effects of drug withdrawal. They may be experiencing chills, vomiting, or diarrhea. They may look and act like zombies. The effects of illicit drugs on the body can be cataclysmic. Remaining engaged when you see this level of suffering while knowing you don't have any tools to remedy it is challenging.

Jail is rarely the answer for these low-level offenders. One of my fiercest weapons has always been the stern look with a raised eyebrow. I'll then extend a firm reprimand. This is my standard response to a negative report or a missed court date or court-ordered appointment. It was the look Ms. Elsa, my mother, gave my brother and me whenever we acted out in public. We knew better. She didn't need words. The eyes alone foretold a major consequence if we didn't get ourselves in order.

In my courtroom, jail was the ultimate punishment, but people knew they were being held to a higher standard than just staying out of lockup. The look conveyed disappointment. And it reinforced what I told people directly: "When you get released without bail, you are out on a Judge Pratt ROR"—released on your own recognizance—"and you represent me and my judgment. Looking at your record, the law says I should hold you to a high bail and send you to the county jail. You don't receive that. Instead, you get an opportunity to go home. So, I expect you to comply with my rules."

Accountability also gave birth to a number of "Judge Pratt-isms." I immediately addressed inappropriate behavior, with any of a number of firm responses:

"You will not come in here and talk to me any kind of way. Your behavior resulted in this court summons, so you will respond to it."

"You don't have to like me, but you will respect this process."

"If you don't want to see me, then don't come to my job. I don't go outside looking for people to come here and give me more work to do. The only way you end up here is when you get a ride from the police."

If a person repeatedly failed to come to court without a plausible excuse, they were held to a bail. Oftentimes I knew that if my court decision came between a drug addict and their next hit, they would unleash a barrage of profanity. When I first started in Part Two court, this happened with predictable regularity. I swear, some days, I would look at my nameplate to ensure no one had etched the word "bitch" into it. After they sobered up, I would see them on video. A person would appear on video in the courtroom when they failed to post their bail or had a bail or a hold from another jurisdiction. I would always begin, "Oh no, before you say one word, you owe this court an apology. You cursed me out in public, and you will apologize publicly." We are not required to take abuse without addressing it.

I also practiced accountability in a way that let defendants know that expectations are high *because* I see their humanity. If people perceive that a judge is being punitive only because of the judge's ego, or because they are dehumanizing the defendant, or because they enjoy being cruel, the offender cannot trust the process. Showing respect can help defendants turn themselves around.

I gave an eighteen-year-old man extra community service days for not showing up to his court-ordered mandates. He spent the whole time complaining to the supervisor about how Judge Pratt didn't like him. "I don't know why Judge Pratt don't like me. She's always on me. She just stays on me about everything. She's on my case more than my mother," he bellyached. And then, as if hearing himself for the first time, he had an epiphany: "Wow . . . she cares about me more than my own mother."

He realized at that moment that holding him accountable was a sign I cared about him. The judge didn't have any animosity toward him. In fact, quite the opposite: she held him in high esteem. Why else would she want him to live up to his full potential? My staying on him, as he called it, made him responsible. It became clear to him that responsibility was precisely what he needed. He needed to pay attention to his actions, and to their consequences. Someone needed to keep him on track. Unfortunately, he felt it didn't happen at home, where he especially needed that level of care.

Another young man, Anton Mansa, came to understand my high standards on punctuality. He knew that being late again would be disrespectful to me. One day, when he was running late to his court-ordered counseling session, he begged the train conductor to record a video explaining that the train was lagging behind. Imagine my surprise when Mr. Mansa arrived in court and raised his cell phone to show me a video of the conductor. The conductor apologized and explained that the train had been delayed. The conductor even added that Mr. Mansa appeared to be a responsible young man, as he had taken an earlier train that would have put him in Newark ahead of his appointment. Mr. Mansa knew I would not be interested in a lame excuse, so he provided proof. I beamed with pride.

So often, after successfully completing Newark Community Solutions or getting sober in a drug program, defendants would say to me, "Thank you for making me do something for myself," or, "I've never been on time so many times in my whole life."

A judge can find it hard not to feel like a cog in the assembly line of justice. We are overwhelmed and overscheduled, to the point where we often ignore the needs of the sickest people who come into our courts. We fail to come up with the proper medication to heal offenders or repair their life circumstances, even when we know that without such an intervention, they will continue to cycle back through the system. It feels obvious to declare that treating people with dignity, respect, and fairness can transform your relationship with them. Restoring a person's sense of dignity throughout the process is critical to repairing our broken judicial system. If the process feels dehumanizing and excessive, the court's relationship with the defendant—and the community—is severed.

Some court professionals, activists, organizers, and politicians still believe, despite the research, that procedural justice is ineffective. I strongly disagree because I've seen the work in practice. I'm not a researcher. I am a judge, and I am talking from years of personal observations. It's true that procedural justice should be responsive to today's community needs. Several cultural and social realities today differ from when the concept of procedural justice was conceived in the 1970s. The country's racial reckoning of 2020 and the social justice movement are a few current factors that need to be taken seriously. Procedural justice is not in opposition to calls for transformative change. There is still value in rehabilitation, alternative sentencing, community partnerships, and addressing recidivism. There is still value in stopping the injustices that occur in our justice system. Shifts in practice to align with procedural justice can happen immediately and have far-reaching impact.

Chapter 2

I HEAR YOU

Ralph G. Nichols, a scholar in the art of listening and the author of thirty books, is also known as the Father of Listening. He said, "The most basic of all human needs is the need to understand and be understood. The best way to understand people is to listen to them."[1] Humans have a profound need to feel that they are being heard and understood. More so than in any other institution, this need to be heard and understood must be met to ensure the proper delivery of justice. If I wanted people in my courtroom to feel that they were being treated with dignity and respect, it was critical that they felt heard. I learned this lesson in a powerful way one day during a court session.

"Well, come on then, motherfucker!" I heard a man yell at his public defender. The public defender attempted to escort the man into the hallway to discuss his case. The defendant, Jimmy Cortado-Clegg, refused to move and continued to disrupt the other court proceedings. He was a sturdily built man in his early thirties with Coolio-style cornrow braids that stretched outward from his head like wiry tree branches. Fuming, he pulled up his sagging pants.

I said, "I know I didn't just hear someone curse in my court-room. I know you did not come into this courtroom with that foolishness. I'm going to suggest you go outside, and before you return you better watch how you speak when you are in this courtroom. Otherwise, you could end up in a cell, headed toward the county jail."

Suddenly a woman, who I later learned was his wife, shouted defiantly, "I wish you would send him to jail!" She crossed her arms across the top of her robust, pregnant belly and stared at me. I was genuinely shocked.

I tilted my head in disbelief, held my breath, and explained not so gently, "Ma'am, they have excellent prenatal services at the county jail, so you can join him in the hallway or in county."

Dressed in a white headwrap and a flowing white shirt, the angry little woman, Joyce Cortado-Clegg, rolled her eyes, heaved up to her feet, and waddled into the hallway while muttering under her breath. Had I checked the lunar calendar on my desk, perhaps I would have been better prepared for the day's insanity.

While I proceeded through the full court calendar, the po-lice officers, court administrator, and prosecutor took turns going into the hallway to counsel the couple. They all re-turned, reporting that there was no getting through to them. They found the two to be combative, abusive, and irrational.

At the end of the court session, I called their case and read them the riot act. I told them that I would not tolerate their disruptive and disrespectful behavior. They sighed, rolled their eyes, and repeatedly interrupted me, which only compounded my frustration at the end of what had been a very long, busy day. The more I corrected them, the more they escalated their irrational behavior. Surprisingly, they had come in on a minor offense—a marijuana possession charge.

When I felt my frustration begin to mix with anger, I decided to take my ego out of the interaction and ask them one question. "Do you two have a problem?" I asked out of desperation.

They lurched forward, papers in hand, and yelled, "That's what we've been trying to tell you!"

I nodded for the officer to pass me what they were trying to present. The husband blurted out, "We lost our daughter!"

The moment the words left his mouth, I recognized him. This guy was the man from a recent news video I had seen. In the clip, he wore the same cornrows and a white tank top, and he was pleading for help. He recounted how he, his wife, and their infant daughter had been inside their home when a drive-by shooting occurred on their street in Irvington, New Jersey. As his wife carried their daughter in her arms, a stray bullet entered their apartment and pierced the baby's body, killing her instantly.

My heart sank into my stomach. In court that day, he explained the distressing details. "Our baby was killed," he said, his angry face softening. The mother's almond-shaped eyes overflowed as tears ran down her copper-colored face. "I lost my job. We can't work. And now we're getting kicked out of our apartment." He said that when the news cameras left, so did the politicians and all their lofty promises of help for him and his family.

I lowered my gaze to hide my tear-filled eyes and said, "I saw you on the NJ.com video two weeks ago talking about this."

The emotion spread through the courtroom like a dark, swift-moving cloud. The feelings of disgust, anger, and sadness were palpable in the air. Some people gasped. Others stopped typing midstroke. The pens ceased moving. It was as if his words had suspended us in midair and forcefully dropped us on our heads. The police officers, all of them fathers, looked down or away. One officer went over and put his hand on Mr. Cortado-Clegg's shoulder. I wondered why God would send these folks to me. How could I possibly help them?

I was the second judge they had appeared before that day. They were offering paperwork documenting their mental health medication to explain their states of mind. Their mental health may not have seemed relevant to their case, but it would have meant the world if someone had listened. No one had listened.

This is the reality for the people who fill our halls of justice. Too many live under the threat of violence and actual violence. The trauma is insurmountable. Support is often nonexistent. We have more sympathy for citizens who live in war-torn countries than we do for fellow Americans who encounter violence daily on our soil.

Unable to see past their pain, the couple in my courtroom that day couldn't hold themselves together or express themselves clearly. They walked around like time bombs, exploding at every interaction with government actors, including the police. In the video, he had pled with the politicians and the government that continued to fail them. They felt abandoned. They were on the verge of homelessness; they had a baby on the way and still hadn't had a chance to mourn the loss of their first child. They hadn't come to terms with the violent tragedy they had endured. They continued to live in the community with the killer, without any leads to his or her capture. There was no justice for them. Their grief had nowhere to go. They had no access to therapy or community support for their trauma. Further punishment was not going to help them.

I immediately assigned them to Newark Community Solutions. I had the social worker come talk to them so they could receive the assistance they needed. Through the program, they could receive counseling and a social worker to facilitate access to resources to help them with their most pressing issues.

Within two weeks, they returned to their court date to introduce their three-day-old child. They were calm. The mom smiled from ear to ear. Once again, I just let them talk, and all of us—the prosecutor, their public defender, the court administrator, the court attendant, the probation officer, and the police officers—listened. They updated me on all the tasks they had been able to accomplish, who had helped them, and what was pending. But most importantly, they gushed over their new miracle. Alethia Parker, the court administrator, beaming, left her seat to hold the baby. The difference between their first and second court appearances was like night and day.

Over the next two years, after they completed the program, they became frequent visitors to my court. They would drop into a session to bring the baby and give us an update, like you would drop in on a family friend. At two years old, the infant looked exactly like her deceased sister. She had even been born on the same day.

They became such a staple in the courtroom that they were able to help other participants. On one occasion, I heard the case of a struggling nineteen-year-old mother who had brought with her a one- and a two-year-old. She didn't have access to child-care. The young children were hungry, and their clothing was wet from drenched diapers. The mom had no dry diapers and no change of clothing with her. The Cortado-Cleggs were in court that day just to visit, and when they saw the young woman in need, they jumped into action by providing her with diapers and a changing pad. The court officer and the probation officer went out to buy the children a change of clothing.

Now, this couple's first court visit could have gone quite differently. Their initial behavior was a clear case of contempt in the face of the court, which warrants jail time. But I made two significant decisions that changed the outcome: (1) I acknowledged that something didn't seem right, and (2) I checked my ego and listened. My listening to them couldn't bring their baby back. It didn't even help the police capture the shooter. However, it gave them something invaluable: a sense of importance. It provided them with a place where people cared about them and would help them through their journey. I imagine it made them feel a little safer.

If these individuals had shown up at work or at a friend's home bleeding from a stab wound, people around them would have insisted that they be rushed to the emergency room and receive treatment. Why shouldn't this commonsense response occur in other situations? Instead, our justice system insists on punishment and only punishment. Folks like the Cortado-Cleggs come into our courtrooms daily, in a similar condition. The justice system demands that we ignore their bleeding and pain and merely move forward, processing their case. How is that justice?

This is the great tragedy of our justice system, the missed opportunity to do good because we are obsessed with punishment. I see a husband who provides his family with shelter and still cannot protect them from injury or death. I see a mother whose arms were created for nurturing and protecting her baby but are still not strong enough to keep her safe. And I see her trepidation and doubt as she fears for another child, still maturing in her belly.

I wonder, *How can I build trust when I'm part of a system that has failed the people in every way imaginable? Do I even have the right to ask for anyone's trust?*

These parents were worthy of our attention, patience, sympathy, care, and love. They didn't receive it from the officer they encountered or the others who couldn't see past their hostility. That hostility was deep-seated in pain and trauma.

Over a year ago, I received a message through my website from Mr. Cortado-Clegg requesting an email address where he could send me pictures of his daughter. He said he was in a good place, with a steady, full-time job. He said he didn't know how to explain to his daughter what I was to her because she already had a godmother, but "You and your court staff and clinic have done more for her than anyone else besides her immediate family."

What makes it so hard for us to hear people? We, the justice system, often cling to the notion that people brought into court are inherently bad. Critics to my approach say, "Why else would the police stop them? They are there for a reason." I'm not advocating that we just give hugs. In "Loving Your Enemies," a sermon from *A Gift of Love*, Dr. Martin Luther King Jr. reminded us, "There is some good in the worst of us and some evil in the best of us."[2] Now, opponents of this position can and will argue, "You want me to focus on the good in a serial killer?" However, they exaggerate when they insist that every individual who comes through the justice system is guilty of mass murder. And this supports my position that we impose our worst assumptions about people who enter the criminal justice system, especially Black and Brown people, and those assumptions become a self-fulfilling prophecy.

***

Hearing a person also requires that you tell them the truth. First you must be willing to listen and hear what is being said behind the actual statements. You may then need to call things out and correct them as needed. Correction can be done out of love. You can't expect people to behave better if they don't receive guidance.

One morning, Mickey Carillo, the police officer who had been with me since day one, approached the bench. Officer Carillo—an energetic Puerto Rican, a Newark native, and a twenty-plus-year veteran officer—had a heart as big as the courtroom. He often advocated on behalf of defendants because he spent so much time counseling them. I sometimes called him "Mr. Public Defender." He hadn't always been that way. In fact, when we started working together, he was quite aggressive toward the people who entered the court. He had started his career on the gang unit and the narcotics task force, chasing down and tackling suspects. When I challenged him to change his approach from an attitude of aggressive law enforcement to one of helping folks get on the right track, it unleashed all his talents. That day, Officer Carillo asked me to call Shirley Tyler's case next. He pointed to the white woman sitting anxiously. "She told me she has an appointment this morning, Judge," Officer Carillo advised as he pled her case.

When I called the case, an emaciated blonde standing over six feet tall approached counsel's table. The courtroom's old-school fluorescent lighting highlighted her chalky complexion and piercing blue eyes. Her resemblance to Elizabeth Montgomery from the TV show *Bewitched* was uncanny. An Elizabeth Montgomery who had been struggling with drug addiction for numerous years, but an Elizabeth Montgomery look-alike nonetheless. Her broad shoulders and height could've made her feel at home on the fashion runways in Milan and Paris. Instead, those shoulders were the only thing that held up the blue and white nursing assistant's uniform that hung loosely from her thin frame. Today her eyes were heavily made up with eyeliner and mascara. She also wore a lightly tinted pink lipstick. I was happy to see that she had put some effort into her look. Maybe she was beginning to feel good about herself once again.

"How's everything going, ma'am?" I inquired before receiving her report.

"I'm really stressed out, Judge," she said in frustration. "I get a call about my son's behavior every day from his kindergarten teacher. The teacher complains that his behavior is out of control and he's real violent in class. I have to meet with the school psychiatrist when I leave here to talk about his behavior and about putting him on medication." She sighed. "I don't know why he behaves like this," she continued in exasperation as she threw her hands up, "and I certainly didn't want him on medications because of the many side effects."

My next question was instinctive, as I had no problem broaching the subject with her. "Did you use while you were pregnant?"

"No, Judge. I stopped when I got pregnant," she responded immediately, her eyes flashing with surprise at the question.

I narrowed my eyes and delved deeper, "Ma'am, so how many months pregnant were you when you stopped using?"

"I stopped the first month," she responded quickly. She had the answer ready before I even asked the question.

I arched my right eyebrow in disbelief. There was a protracted silence. You could see the folks in the audience lower their gaze while shaking their heads. Some even covered their mouths to suppress a chuckle. *Game recognizes game*, I thought as I watched people react. The addicts in the room recognized the lie immediately. It still caught me by surprise, however, so it took me a moment to reply. Most *sober* women don't know they are pregnant in the first month. I found it highly unlikely that a woman in the grips of addiction would know, especially since I had her criminal record in front of me.

The number of visibly pregnant women arrested and then brought out of the cellblock to appear before me was staggering. They were arrested on prostitution or drug charges or both. I recall one pregnant woman whom I gave bail and sent to the county jail. She had a crack cocaine possession charge, and owed money on a recent guilty plea to another drug possession charge. At five months pregnant, her belly was so low it looked as if the baby were trying to escape her body. When I later saw her via video from the county jail, she said that the jail had sent her directly to the hospital, where she was told that her baby was dead. The doctor said she might have died as well if she hadn't been sent to the hospital.

So, in talking to Ms. Tyler, I could have let it go. *Mind your business*, I tried to tell myself. However, there was a lot at stake here. We know, and research has laid bare, that exposure to drugs while in the womb has long-lasting consequences to the fetus, namely, impaired brain development and function.[3] Ms. Tyler's attempt to shield herself from responsibility was negating the truth about her son's condition. So, no. Letting it go—not an option.

In response to her claim that she had stopped using drugs during the first month of pregnancy, I looked her in the eye and said, "Ma'am, I don't believe you." Then I continued to write on the file.

Stunned and taken aback, she stammered, "No, no, Judge. Really, I . . . I . . . I did stop using during my pregnancy." Her eyes widened, refusing to blink.

"I heard you, ma'am. I said, I don't believe you," I enunciated slowly.

The drama intensified as she shook her head back and forth, her eyes now blinking like a flickering light bulb. Unwilling to back down, she repeated herself and offered one convoluted statement after the other to convince me.

Finally, I stopped her. I wanted to sound authoritative without sounding harsh, so I said, "Let me say this to you, ma'am. That wall that you have built up to stop the pain from the truth is the same wall that's going to stop your son from receiving the help he needs. When you tell this story of being clean during your pregnancy, the psychiatrist doesn't get a full family history for your son. So today, when you go speak to that psychiatrist, I want you to lay everything on the table. Tell him the truth so he can help your son."

Her response, when she finally offered it, was a soft "Okay." Her eyes filled with tears, and she lowered her gaze.

She shared that she'd been addicted for about fifteen years, and her criminal record supported this report. Her son was five years old. She had been telling herself the lie about not using during her pregnancy for so long that she had begun to believe it. Unfortunately, the lie prevented the school officials from having a complete and accurate medical history of the young boy, impeding their ability to treat him. By asking her to face the truth, I allowed the court to help her sort out this false story that she had held on to. In protecting herself, she was hurting her son. And they both needed healing. I often shared a saying in court: "People who love you tell you the truth. Even when it hurts."

In this case, hearing Ms. Tyler required the listener to extend compassion, sympathy, and empathy. I needed to be honest with her so that she could help her son. She needed to leave the conversation with her dignity intact. Humiliating and attacking her would have closed her mind to the necessary message.

In the courtroom, ensuring that a person is heard often requires the judge to practice the art of shutting up. You can then listen intently and read between the lines. I had a case involving an eighteen-year-old high school student, initially charged with possession of an unlawful weapon, whose case was transferred from the superior court to the municipal court. The police charged her with carrying a knife in her purse as she went through the metal detector at her high school, which is an indictable offense with a possible prison sentence. The charge was later reduced to a disorderly persons offense and sent down to the municipal court, which is how she ended up before me.

In New Jersey's criminal justice system, we've decided to treat our children—yes, I'm calling them children—as adults once they turn eighteen and violate the law. As a result, they end up in adult court for minor offenses. The grown-ups have determined that this chronological age somehow plants our young people into adulthood. The Newark public school district has eighteen high schools, which includes charter high schools. Now, when eighteen-year-old students engage in behavior that would typically land them in the principal's office, the schools' zero-tolerance policies ensure they end up before a judge. These policies have stripped the schools' principals of disciplinary and reconciliatory authority. The behavior is deemed a criminal offense, and it gets them processed in the criminal justice system.

What is most disturbing to me is that we often have more police stationed in our high schools than guidance counselors. Imagine what this tells our children. Mainly, we are telling them that their postgraduation success is of less interest to us than policing and incarcerating their bodies now.

The girl who'd been brought in on a downgraded weapons charge that was now a disorderly persons charge, Aminah Snipes, sat with her friend in the front row, loudly giggling about whatever high school girls giggle about. I did not like their playful manner, so I gave them a stern look and said, "If you are sitting in my courtroom, it is serious business. I need all the giggling to stop. Now."

When I called young Ms. Snipes's case, she bounced up to counsel's table in an oversized pink sweatshirt that muted her pale, light brown skin and hung on her less-than-ninety-pound frame. Her long bangs covered the top of her almond-shaped face. She looked totally out of place in the courtroom. Like a baby.

I asked, "And where is the parent? Where's the adult?"

She responded as the tears flowed down her cheeks, "My mom didn't come today."

I sent her case to Newark Youth Court, a program for young people ages ten to nineteen, established by the city of Newark and the Newark Municipal Court in partnership with the

Center for Court Innovation. The center operates similar programs throughout New York City, in Harlem, Queens, Staten Island, and the Bronx. Youth court offers a restorative justice approach to youthful misconduct that would otherwise result in suspension, expulsion, or even juvenile detention or jail.

At the Newark Youth Court, a jury of Ms. Snipes's peers, local high school students trained to hear low-level cases, would resolve her matter. These fellow students are youth court members. Since youth court is a restorative justice practice, it doesn't involve state criminal prosecution. Instead, one of the teens, the community advocate, who represents the interests of the community, presents the harm caused to the community by the offending young person's behavior. The offending young person is represented by the respondent's advocate, like a public defender, who presents the defendant's position to the jury members. After asking questions and deliberating, the jury imposes sanctions that might include attending a workshop, participating in community service, or serving as a juror on another case.

Once she completed the program, Ms. Snipes returned to my court to read an essay. My natural inclination was to lecture her. However, I decided to practice the art of shutting up, so I just listened.

As she stood before me reading her essay, her voice and hands trembling, she said, "Judge, I'm so sorry I had that knife. I never intended to hurt anyone, and I'm really sorry. It's just that I'm scared all the time. I'm scared when I walk to school in the morning. I'm scared when I walk home in the afternoon. I'm scared when I walk in my old neighborhood. I'm scared at night. So, I barricade myself in my bedroom, and I sleep with the knife under my pillow."

We had failed her. The adults were responsible for providing her with a sense of safety. Instead, she had been walking around with a knife to protect herself.

For people who see their job as a calling, it's impossible to leave work at the door. When I arrived home that evening, I repeatedly heard Ms. Snipes say, "I barricade myself in my room and sleep with the knife under my pillow." Why was she doing this?

I later called the social worker and asked her to follow up. We discovered that Ms. Snipes's mother's boyfriend was sexually molesting her. This young person walked into a school where she encountered police officers daily and didn't trust them enough to report the molestation. Instead, she only got their attention when she took measures to protect herself with a household kitchen knife.

If societies are judged by how they treat the most vulnerable, think about what it means that we respond to a young girl's sexual trauma by charging her with a criminal offense. She should have been able to tell her story before she resorted to carrying a knife for protection. She should have been allowed to tell her story to the police when she was caught with the knife. She should have never met me.

A report titled *The Sexual Abuse to Prison Pipeline: The Girls' Story* states that although no national data exist, local and regional studies consistently show that girls who end up in juvenile justice systems have disproportionately been the victims of sexual abuse. In California, 81 percent of detained girls reported that they had experienced past sexual and physical abuse. In South Carolina, the figure was 81 percent, and in Oregon it was 93 percent.[4]

Girls are usually arrested for low-level crimes—most commonly running away, abusing substances, or truancy. In nearly all cases, they engaged in the violations in order to survive sexual abuse. And what is our justice system's response? It further victimizes them by criminalizing and punishing them.

Research shows that girls of color are significantly affected by this practice. Even though African American girls, like Ms. Snipes, make up only a small percentage of the US population, they represent 35 percent of the girls who are held and sentenced in our restrictive, corrections-patterned juvenile jail system.[5] Native American girls are also overrepresented in juvenile corrections facilities, reflecting 3 percent of the girls in detention. Despite the glaring evidence that sexual victimization of girls leads to their entering the juvenile justice system, the system typically overlooks abuse incidents.[6]

Fortunately for Ms. Snipes, her case was dismissed. From the beginning, the prosecutor did not believe that hers was a case that should be pursued. The public defender requested an expedited expungement of the arrest and its dismissal from her record. The court case manager received an update from the school social worker, who asked for the sexual molestation allegations to be formalized. Some of the adults in this young person's life were now living up to their responsibility to protect her. Unfortunately, other young people slip through the cracks, and their trauma dictates their future.

* * *

I came to the practice of assigning essays because I found that people search far and wide for answers that actually lie inside of them. Judge Alex Calabrese from the Red Hook Community

Justice Center was the first judge I observed using personal essays as a technique to give defendants a voice in the court process. He asked defendants to write about their circumstances and turn the paper in at their next court proceeding. He read the essay and discussed it with the individual.

I have the opportunity and privilege to discuss my reforms with legal practitioners around the world. At one point I made a series of presentations in Scotland to the judiciary and other agencies. During a reception, I took a deep dive into the utility of essays in an informal talk with a small group of judges. Weeks after my return home, the defense attorney who had organized the events there forwarded another defense attorney's email to my attention.

While sitting in a sheriff's court (in Scotland, most judges are called sheriffs), the defense counsel wrote that she had observed an unusual exchange between the judge and the attorneys. The judge was presiding over a case in which the defendant had been released from prison five weeks prior. The defendant, who suffered from drug addiction, had produced yet another positive drug test. They discussed performing a drug treatment and testing order (DTTO) assessment. The DTTO assessment is conducted prior to an order for treatment, which is intended to offer a long-term solution to the defendant's underlying drug problem. Previous assessments had been unsuccessful, and the defendant continued to fail the drug tests.

The observing defense counsel was surprised when the judge engaged in a lengthy discussion directly with the defendant about her situation. The judge then mentioned in open court that he'd recently had a conversation with an American judge who had more experience dealing with drug-use cases than he had.

The observing defense counsel wrote, "Following the example the American judge gave in her talk, the magistrate judge set the accused a homework assignment to write 500 words on where she sees the case going." The email noted how unusual this was, and concluded, "It's a sign of good things to come for presiding with kindness!"

The judge not only conversed directly with the defendant; he used the assignment of an essay as a device to engage her in her own recovery. Sobriety couldn't be achieved through punishment alone—the defendant had to take agency over her own life and over her own role in overcoming addiction.

Drug addicts may struggle to take the time to be introspective when all they want is to be numb and to make excuses for their behavior. Their perspective can be narrowed to their immediate cravings. But when they are assigned to write an essay, the process is like taking truth serum. They begin to think about what is driving the behavior that causes them to end up in court.

Initially, defendants in my court who were assigned essays would begrudgingly jot down a couple of sentences that they thought would get me off their backs. Yet I knew that the process of thinking through a topic and writing an essay could be cathartic. And most importantly, I needed folks to participate and become invested in their own healing and transformation. Sitting high on my perch and merely ordering them to change their behavior would have no impact. They needed to identify and address the lies, the memories, and the traumas that compelled them to want to numb themselves.

Contrary to what many assume, my asking people to read their essays aloud was not meant to humiliate them. Instead, it was an attempt to empower them. Reading their work product aloud also raised the stakes. In the beginning, I struggled to decipher their handwriting and the meaning of their essays. Many of the authors were the products of inept school systems and suffered cognitive issues, to say nothing of how prolonged illicit drug use impacts the brain. When I asked them to read their essays aloud, they took pride in what they wrote. Young men didn't want to look bad in a room of their peers. Pride in their work—coupled with the fact that I would send them into the hallway to rewrite their essay if they tried to pass off some half-baked foolishness—significantly improved the quality of the work. I believed folks had something significant to say because there was value in their experiences. And I knew those experiences could help others who were similarly situated or headed down the same path.

I was often asked why I would assign such a difficult task to the particular population of individuals who showed up in my courtroom. My response was always, "Imagine how little I would have to think of them to believe they couldn't express their thoughts or didn't have the right to express them." The essays were not about me trying to get into people's business. They were about helping them resolve their own business.

I see people who love their children deeply, but whose pain from years of trauma runs equally deep. I saw this in the case of a thirty-something, Irish, red-headed, red-faced, drug-addicted mother, Claire McFay. I assigned her an essay titled "A Letter to My Daughter." After sharing the details of her childhood living with a drug-addicted father, Ms. McFay wrote, "My drug addiction is not about my lack of love for you, but about my lack of love for myself." She continued, "Learning that is the only thing that I'm grateful to this addiction for." Ms. McFay never understood her own father's addiction, and

I cautioned her that she might send her daughter on the same quest for answers if she didn't get clean and stay clean.

Other essay topics also offer value. Writing "A Letter to My Teenage Self" gives the author the opportunity to be reflective and to hear the advice they failed to heed as adults. The topic "If I Believed One Positive Thing About Myself, How Would My Life Be Different?" requires the writer to think of their redeeming qualities for two weeks before they return to court. What a shift in perspective. I wasn't trying to teach them the fundamentals of positive thinking, because that alone will not change their circumstances. It was getting them to understand that they were just one mental shift away from rising out of the haze. Maybe if a young woman believed she was worthy of love, she would remember that she once had hopes and aspirations before becoming a career heroin-addicted prostitute. Perhaps she could remember somebody in her life who had shown her affection. Maybe she could remember some pleasant moments before the grandmother's or mother's death that had sent her life spiraling downward.

In many cases, the simple act of having their story heard could bring about better outcomes. While reading their essay in court, a person may have felt that, for the first time in their life, people were listening to them.

And we were listening. We listened to young African American men dissect and analyze the essay written by Kiese Laymon titled "How to Kill Yourself and Others Slowly in America," from his book of the same name, which I sometimes assigned to defendants.[7] The men reading the essay could relate to Laymon's sentiment that young Black men are born on parole in America, unable to make one mistake. He writes about being suspended from college in Mississippi for one year for taking a book out of the library without checking it out, even though he returned it the next day. We listened to a father pour his heart out in "A Letter to My Son," who was sitting in prison just like he had. In some cases, they were writing to their deceased son.

Often, essays reveal vital information that helps the court give the defendant the resources they need to redirect cycles of self-destructive behavior. Some essays show that a person has been trapped in a misunderstanding about themselves, a lie that has led to years of self-abuse and unlawful activity. This was the case for Raquel Loops, a forty-something-year-old heroin-addicted woman who arrived in court to read her essay accompanied by two family members. It was quite typical for people to invite others to court to hear them read their essays. They did so for moral support, but also because they were proud of their effort.

Ms. Loops, a portly African American woman, leaned on a cane as she stood up. Wincing, she struggled down the row toward the aisle and hobbled toward counsel's table. Her pain seemed to surge with every step. As she adjusted her church-lady glasses, I could see her hand shaking like a leaf.

"You are only reading your essay to me," I reassured her with a smile.

She unfolded the yellow legal-size pages. And then she read the most powerful line I had ever heard in court: "I've been suffering from a fatal disease for twenty-four years." Her essay described her diagnosis with lupus, a painful and incurable disease that in severe cases can be lethal. It led to feelings of hopelessness, which opened the floodgates to depression. Then

came depression's partner, bad decision-making, which resulted in her self-medicating with heroin—and ultimately the
heroin possession charge that had brought her to court.

Ms. Loops finished reading to thunderous applause. We
were moved by her honesty and relatability. She had expressed
the deep pain shared by so many people sitting in the courtroom that day, waiting to have their cases heard. Her story
didn't contain a single line about a desire to violate or even
disregard the law. It was the story of a human being dealing
with a death sentence.

As she removed her glasses to wipe her eyes, I asked her,
"Ma'am, do you know that you beat that disease in the first
year? You can't have a fatal disease for twenty-four years. You
stared down death and won. Every day you wake up and live,
you defiantly tell that disease, 'I wish you would come for me!
You can't have my life.'" She looked at me in shock. She had
never thought of her situation from that perspective.

I continued, "You have been telling yourself the wrong
story. You've been telling yourself a story where you're the
victim, when actually you are the victor. Yes, you have to fight
the disease, but every day at the end of the fight, you're still
here." As she walked away from counsel's table, I noticed she
walked a little straighter and with a little less pain. Maybe it
was just me.

I thought about Ms. Loops for some time after her fines
were vacated. The news of her diagnosis, and the fact that there
was no cure for her condition, had made her vulnerable to
seeking the numbness that heroin guarantees. Didn't her health
care provider have a responsibility to assist her in coping with
the initial shock of the diagnosis? Lupus can be manageable
in many cases, but for some it can be life threatening, and the

uncertainty can be frightening. There was a causal connection between her underlying medical condition and her drug addiction. If her medical condition had given rise to the feelings of hopelessness that triggered the drug use, then I, as a person in authority, could use hope and facts to help drive the process of healing.

Writing and presenting essays requires those who come before the court to contemplate their situation and deal with their emotions. This process was an eye-opener for Adrian Satchell, who finally linked every bad thing that had happened to him as an adult to a fateful trip to the basketball court thirty years earlier. He had been arrested on a heroin possession charge. He had failed to return to court after his initial summons and was full of excuses. His family didn't help, as they were enablers who supported his excuses. I assigned him an essay titled "If I Knew Then What I Know Now, How Would My Life Be Different?" Turns out I would be the one who would find his backstory illuminating.

A well-dressed man in his late forties, with curly, thinning hair that was carefully styled, Mr. Satchell came from a good family and had had plans to join the military as a teen. Back then, he also fancied himself a rapper, so he carried a book bag containing a black-and-white composition notebook full of rhymes. He and three friends spent countless hours at the basketball court improving their game, trying to "be like Mike," as the saying went, referring to legendary Chicago Bulls player Michael Jordan.

One particular day, he and his friends were headed to the basketball court, joking and bragging about their skills. They encountered a book bag in their path. They took the bag into an alley and searched its contents. It contained a stack of cash and a handgun. They decided to divvy up the money and get rid of the bag. Mr. Satchell took the gun and placed it in his book bag. They proceeded to the basketball court, which surprisingly was empty. While they were playing, the older neighborhood guys arrived, ready to start trouble as usual. They told Mr. Satchell and his friends to get off the court and started roughing them up. Two of the bullies attacked one of Mr. Satchell's friends, and he yelled, "Get off of him, man!"

The ringleader turned his attention toward Mr. Satchell. "You always carrying that book bag. Give it to me. You gotta have something in it." The teen warned the older guy to stay away. But the bully continued to approach him. Emboldened by the weapon in his bag, Mr. Satchell reached for it, meaning to scare the bully. *Bang!* A shot rang out.

His essay didn't reveal what happened immediately after he fired the shot, but it did say that he was charged with a criminal offense. As he and his father anxiously awaited the results of his case, his fear of prison drove him down the wrong road. He began doing drugs and getting into more trouble. By the time he received probation on the case with the gun, he had picked up multiple new charges due to behavior that had resulted from his remorse and anxiety. His dreams of becoming a soldier were dashed, as were his chances of obtaining gainful employment.

The person who stood before me was a broken middle-aged man who relived a single traumatic moment every time he got high and every time he did something to get money for drugs. Thirty years later, he was still battling his drug addiction and brooding over why he hadn't just taken the money and left the gun. Writing and presenting the essay was a profound expression of regret for Mr. Satchell. He grieved how that one choice had stolen his youth and his hopes for the future. Even though the state had never imposed a prison sentence for his actions, he had built a prison for himself in his own mind and given himself a perpetual sentence.

Yes, the story served as a cautionary tale for the young people in the courtroom that day who might have been headed down a similar wayward path. However, what was most important about the essay was what it revealed to me. It illuminated the distinction between the consequences of youthful missteps made by people who live in urban areas and the consequences of missteps made by young people who live in the suburbs. In poor, urban, Black and Brown communities that are overrun with crime, unemployment, and health disparities, the chances that an abandoned bag contains contraband is high. That means a young person's misjudgment in keeping the bag will lead to more significant consequences that will steer them to encounters with the criminal justice system. Racially segregated, working-class neighborhoods often lack resources and support, frequently trapping their residents in intergenerational poverty and imposing limited choices and opportunities on young people. Lamentably, those limitations dictate the considerable dangers they face, even when engaging in everyday youthful activities.

***

Reading essays aloud in court gives defendants an opportunity to be heard, and the applause afterward shows, loudly, that we have heard them. The power of applause is about acknowledgment. It's about what happens when people believe that their story, their humanity, is being recognized. In my court, we used applause to create connections and to show appreciation for a person's efforts. Praising individuals in court for even the slightest accomplishment can be deeply significant and motivating. We clapped when someone reported getting a new job. We clapped when a son and mother hugged after he'd proven that his behavior had turned around. We clapped when a participant completed the Newark Community Solutions program or signed up for a GED course. We clapped when a person had a few months, weeks, or days clean. We even clapped when a person reported taking their mental health medication regularly. This acknowledgment shifted everyone's thinking. And don't forget that we were clapping—celebrating the individual—in a place designed for judgment and punishment.

Motivation, even for taking the smallest steps on the right path, can be life changing. One day, a homeless man with schizophrenia finally agreed to participate in Newark Community Solutions after numerous attempts by a staffer to persuade him to. He said, "Judge, I'm going to do this program so that I can be one of those jokers you clap for."

I have been known to admonish an entire courtroom for failing to properly applaud a young person who has graduated from high school: "Hold on. We can throw a party for a person who comes home from prison, but we can't clap for this young person who just graduated from high school? That's why the community is on its head. We are going to try this again. We are better than that."

Atim Maxwell had been difficult from the start. Nineteen years old and cocky, he was a revered former high school football star who had received a full scholarship to a college in Virginia. He'd dropped out after his first year and now stood in front of me on a charge of hindering the administration of justice. In plain English, he had cursed out a cop.

Mr. Maxwell was full of excuses and in a state of perpetual anger. There are times in court when leniency is required; this was not one. I cut him no slack. He needed to get back on track, and quickly. I could not have him out in the community warring with the police. It was not going to end well. When I asked him why he had dropped out of college, he blamed everyone else. When I asked about his plans for the future, he thought he could finesse me. He soon learned that "Judge Pratt don't play," and she couldn't be finessed. When he was late or missed an appointment, I accepted no excuses and gave him additional community service days. I readily utilized the stern reprimand. I was inflexible with Mr. Maxwell because I knew he could do so much more than he was doing. I needed him to understand that. I especially didn't want him to end up like the former high school star athletes that came through my courtroom with drug charges.

One day he stood before me, ready for battle, with his usual scowl, jaw clenched, left hand grabbing right wrist, shoulders squared. I half smiled and asked, "Why are you so angry?"

As he went through his extensive list of grievances, I heard the subtext. I asked, "This is all about Dad, isn't?"

He rolled his eyes and sucked his teeth. I took that as a yes and said, "Well, that's your essay. You are going to write a letter to your father and tell him how you feel."

When Mr. Maxwell returned to court and began reading his essay, you could hear the arms of a wristwatch move. He asked his father why he hadn't seen him in five years even though the man lived in Newark. He told his father how he had stood up for him and defended him when his mother and grandmother spoke ill of him, even though they were right. He finished by saying, "And even after you have done all these things to me, I still got love for you."

The courtroom erupted in resounding applause. The attorneys, the staff, the officers, and, most importantly, the spectators clapped. Mr. Maxwell's beaming smile radiated pure pride. Then he took a slight bow—what a ham. An officer walked up to him to pat him on the back and congratulate him. As he floated out of the courtroom, audience members gave him approving nods and shook his hand. On this particular day Mayor Ras Baraka was visiting to see the community court at work. A longtime champion of criminal justice reform and restorative justice practices, he had voted as a councilman to support the program and continued to support it in his role as mayor. Unbeknownst to us, he was also Mr. Maxwell's former high school principal, and he knew the young man's father. The mayor later remarked to the staff, "You all are doing God's work in there. It felt more like a classroom than a courtroom."

I remember a twenty-one-year-old man with schizophrenia who stood before me, twisting the bleached-blond streak at the front of his afro mohawk. His onyx-colored complexion and the pure white of his eyes gave him a soft, childlike appearance. He took quite the journey through my courtroom. He came to court on the wrong days. He looked at me with dazed eyes when I reprimanded him for missing appointments with his counselor. After working on a system to get him to his appointments on time, he began to make progress, including enrolling in a six-month mental health program. One day, he came to court dressed up in slacks and a button-down shirt. At the announcement that he'd completed the program, the courtroom's applause was deafening. He slowly flashed a shy smile and lowered his gaze. Everyone was elated, but perhaps also lamenting that they would no longer be a part of his progress.

I told him, "I'm really proud of you for getting through this."

He smiled again and said, "I'm proud of myself, Judge."

These examples illustrate the importance of acknowledgment. When a person hears applause from strangers, it serves as recognition. Perhaps they have never received encouragement like that before, people recognizing their efforts—and their worth. Cheering for someone is a minor act that can produce major positive outcomes. Applause says, "We have listened to you, and we were moved by what you said." It is the highest form of approval.

When a person believes they have been heard, it makes them feel as if they matter. It is crucial that a person who is facing consequences believe that their life matters to the powerful individuals who are making decisions about their fate. Fairness cannot be achieved in the judicial system without both parties acknowledging that the defendant has worth. This is particularly true when making findings of guilt or innocence.

People will say, "If you were arrested by the police, you did something." Judges, neutral arbiters of the facts, must hear the evidence presented as if the arrest is of no consequence. We must hear what is being said, setting aside our own prejudice. We must remove our egos from the equation and truly listen. And to listen we must give defendants an opportunity to speak. This may require tools, like the essay, that allow people to speak unencumbered.

Chapter 3

I SEE YOU

As the saying goes, "Be curious, not judgmental." I'll modify it as a principle for judges: "Be curious while you are judging." True delivery of justice requires being curious about the information before us. And that curiosity requires us to see both what is obvious and what is not so obvious, what is there and what's not easily apparent.

You can understand the value of this lesson in the case of defendant Michael Kareem. Hoisting his sagging jeans, he approached counsel's table and grimaced. Then he stood motionless, his eyes open unnaturally wide. I could see the indentation around his hairline from the wave cap he had been wearing before he walked into the courtroom. Athletically built and no older than twenty, Mr. Kareem towered a full foot over the court resource coordinator, Janet Idrogo, whose responsibilities included reading the compliance report.

As she read aloud, I blinked in bewilderment. I wondered, *Why is this report extensive and, once again, negative?* I noticed that the defendant was mumbling under his breath. *Did I catch a curse word?*

I chided him with a raised eyebrow. "Oh, no. We don't curse here. This is not a problem that I caused."

I shook my head as Idrogo continued to itemize his infractions. It was like listening to the terrible lyrics of a song replayed ad nauseam on the radio: he had failed to show up to his group session, he had missed an individual session, he was a no-show to community service, twice. As she read, he looked away, continued to mumble, and flared his nostrils.

Something strange was happening. I felt it in my gut. Mr. Kareem's demeanor was all wrong for someone who was about to get in trouble with Judge-Pratt-Don't-Play. His reaction to this terrible report was absolute indifference. He didn't take exception to anything she said. He didn't interrupt her. He didn't object. There was no "Check it, Judge, check it. Let me tell you what really went down," or the customary "What had happened was. . . ." (When I heard that, I always interrupted by saying, "Anytime I hear, 'What had happened was . . . ,' it should be followed with, 'Once upon a time, in a land far, far, away.' Watch where you're going with this story.") He didn't even appear contrite.

He began to rock from left to right. He pulled up his slipping jeans. He nervously placed his hands in his pockets and removed them. He repeatedly looked around the courtroom. He, however, did not look at me.

I prepared to take him to task with my usual battery of questions. "How many times are you supposed to get a second chance?" "You don't have to do this program, but you will have to do your jail time." "Why can't you show up?" But as I looked closer, I saw his eyes go from an untroubled, emotionless, blank stare to a furious red scowl. And it was those eyes that worried me. They were wide and unbalanced. I looked at the officers, who could also tell that something was not right. One officer moved closer to Mr. Kareem to see if his presence would calm him. Mr. Kareem and I locked eyes, and I waited for him to say something.

He finally responded. What we didn't know was that we were lawn chairs unprepared for a tornado. His breathing became heavy and loud as he raised and lowered his shoulders like Bruce Banner when he transforms into the Incredible Hulk. I stared in amazement at the metamorphosis. He began screaming and flailing his long arms. "Just shoot me! Go ahead! Just kill me!" He turned his body from left to right to face the officers on either side of him. His shouts filled the room, along with audible gasps from the court audience.

I felt a sense of disbelief as I watched this young man suffer a disturbing breakdown in the front of the courtroom. He had come to court wanting suicide by police. He taunted the officers, lunging toward them and yelling, "Shoot me! Go ahead and shoot me!"

Instead, the two officers attempted to diffuse the situation by removing him from the courtroom. He thrashed around like a fish out of water. He wore an ominous just-let-me-die look. The officers lifted him off the ground and carried him into the cellblock. He tussled with them and reached for one of the officers' guns.

What personal crisis could be so dire that this young man would want to end his life in this way? The lives of people who appeared before me were constantly in flux. They endured poverty-induced unsteadiness, unpredictability, and instability, the constant threat of violence, and the psychological stress of racism. Honestly, I don't know how folks survive it all.

In 2018, the Centers for Disease Control and Prevention recorded that 2,406 African American males died by suicide.[1] According to the American Association of Suicidology, risk factors that lead to suicide for African American men include, but are not limited to, psychological stress, access to weapons, exposure to racial discrimination, family dysfunction, and inadequate coping skills.[2] Guns have been the primary means used by Black men in the United States to commit suicide. In light of the data, and in light of all I've seen, should I have been surprised that a confluence of issues would drive this young man to attempt a violent and public suicide?

The social worker came down to the courtroom to perform an initial assessment of Mr. Kareem's state. One officer called the hospital's crisis unit as the other officer talked to him. I tried to catch my breath. I had to continue with my calendar. The courtroom was still full of individuals who had to be heard, and the best thing to do was get them out of court.

At the end of the session, I asked the officers to bring Mr. Kareem back into the courtroom. He had calmed down considerably. He had told one officer that everything had been going wrong for him over the past couple of weeks. The court mandates were just one more thing that he couldn't accomplish. He said he didn't want to live anymore. He just wanted to end it all. He didn't see another way out.

There are countless reasons that Black men don't seek assistance—that is, treatment for mental health issues like depression. A significant reason is the stigma associated with admitting you have a mental health issue.[3] For many young men, bravado and toughness are essential survival skills necessary to fend off aggressors in their communities. Being labeled mentally ill makes them incredibly vulnerable. They believe it would be like putting a bull's-eye on their back at a firing range. They could become a walking target.

Mr. Kareem reminded me of another young man in his twenties who had participated in the Newark Community Court program, Eduardo Gonzales. In his late twenties, he was tall, gaunt, pale, with dark circles around his puffy eyes. Suffering from mental and emotional exhaustion, he had turned himself in to the police on a traffic warrant. He had ventured into the wrong neighborhood and sold drugs, and someone had put a $1,000 bounty on his head through Facebook. Through his public defender, the prosecutor, and his outreach counselor, he asked that I send him to the county jail for protection. He had been running for three days, including hiding out in the McDonald's downtown. He was afraid for his life. His bad decision-making had created his present dilemma—he had violated both the law and the rules of the streets—and he had ended up at the courthouse for help.

Some cynics will say I'm suggesting they use a "third eye" when doing their job. I'm imploring them to look more closely at the circumstances leading up to a defendant's chaotic behavior. We have to be more perceptive. We need to look behind what we may be hearing and seeing. When Mr. Kareem's behavior didn't align with the context of the situation, I had to look deeper, and most importantly I had to remain calm. His bulging eyes, his body language, his movements—all were warning signs. I would have missed critical details of what was happening with Mr. Kareem if I had only listened to the report without observing him. And that could have produced a disastrous alternative outcome for him.

Instead of being frightened by his outburst, I was prepared. I expected him to have a peculiar response when he finally spoke, even though I was alarmed by his words. If I hadn't been paying attention, I might have panicked and jumped off the bench for safety, as judges are instructed to do. This would have signaled the police officers to go into security lockdown mode. They would have restrained him by throwing him to the floor to ensure my safety. Instead, the officers and the entire court went into triage mode. He was safely lifted off the floor and carried into the back. The social worker and the hospital were called simultaneously. Nothing could have prevented Mr. Kareem's breakdown because it had started before he arrived to court. However, responding to it based on our observations that he was having an emotional meltdown—not engaging in an act of violence—created the safest outcome for him.

We need to consider the societal context of an individual before doling out punishment for what appears to be inappropriate behavior in our courtrooms. It is critical to know that societal factors such as threats of violence, previous encounters with police, and community dangers influence how people feel and respond when they enter court. This young man's distraught and hysterical reaction signaled an emotional or mental breakdown. His compromised condition also explained his inability to comply with specific court orders. Identifying and addressing these underlying issues would be crucial in ensuring compliance and providing him with the necessary counseling services to help him. Yet the kneejerk reaction to his behavior would have been to hold him in contempt of court. Holding a person in contempt and subsequently jailing them is the tool judges have been trained to use to maintain control of their courtrooms. It is woefully inadequate for most situations.

I converted Mr. Kareem's court requirements to counseling sessions as a part of his sentence. Increasing the frequency of his sessions allowed him to build a relationship with a therapist whom he could continue to see even after completing his other mandates. It also allowed him to develop and continue his relationship with the officers who spared him on that fateful day. He began to show up for his counseling appointments and ultimately completed the program. He was connected to counseling services in the community. He later apologized to the officers. He was starting to feel like himself again.

***

A sense of curiosity will also help you look deeper, as in the case of Wilamina Williams. "Judge, you saw me. That made all the difference," she reflected later during an interview. "When you're lost, when you're totally lost out there, you need someone to still see you."

On the day she first came to court, I watched as lies and excuses dripped with ease from her full, pouty lips. It was like hearing her say, "The devil made me do it." Accountability is hard to find in the world of the addict. I've observed that once a person becomes a drug addict, they sprout a lie chromosome. Lying is a trait that appears in their personality and becomes dominant. And every time you communicate with them, you are made keenly aware of it. It becomes their most apparent character flaw. Even though they practice lying with persistence, they remain horrible at it. The lies are more often than not nonsensical, usually comical, and without fail annoying.

I sat there stone-faced, watching Ms. Williams perform. Her round, cocoa-brown face had a smooth, unblemished complexion, uncommon among the women on the prostitution stroll. Her fake ponytail drooped, half detached, and shifted to the left side of her head. Ms. Williams, I noticed, looked incredibly healthy and clean compared to the women she'd been arrested with the day before. She exuded spark and charisma as she yammered meaningless words through an oddly radiant smile. After a while, her mounting excuses for missing her court dates began to sound like Charlie Brown's teacher in the animated versions of Charles M. Schulz's *Peanuts* comics.

I probably let her carry on longer than I should have, but I wanted to watch her climb out of the hole she'd dug for herself. I was curious about her creativity and charisma. I saw beyond her lies. She was astute and had held on to many positive remnants of her old life. She was also very respectfully persistent. I remained motionless as she tried to ingratiate herself to me. Her public defender's attempts to interrupt her were futile.

"Enough. This ends today," I said sternly. "Either you go upstairs and do the program, or you can have your suspended jail sentence. And you'll receive your jail time every time you come back here. I only have jail time or assistance to offer you. If you don't want the assistance, that's fine, but you will have to do your jail time."

Ms. Williams began to work closely with her assigned social worker to receive assistance tailored to her needs. For the first time, she felt comfortable enough to confide to her social worker that she heard voices inside her head. The social worker found her a shelter and paired her with the Community Psychiatric Institute to treat her co-occurring schizophrenia and drug addiction.

She told me she had started smoking marijuana to deal with the voices, but it was not enough. They just got louder, so she turned to crack. This was in the 1980s, when the flood of crack cocaine was devouring Black communities. Throughout her life, Ms. Williams had conversed with the voices in her head as they comforted her through the repeated episodes of sexual assault she endured from her uncles and father. The voices stepped in when she became overwhelmed. Then she was sexually assaulted as an adult, and everything changed. "The rape, the rape. I couldn't shut down the voices from that rape. They became mean and would say, 'You're dirty, you got what you deserved, just kill yourself.'"

During Ms. Williams's time in the Newark Community Solutions program, I assigned her an essay titled "A Letter to My Son." He had died suddenly from an undiagnosed condition. When she read the essay aloud in court, she experienced a catharsis. The courtroom burst into applause as she lowered her gaze and clutched the pages.

"Reading that essay in the courtroom, I surrendered. I finally accepted that I would not see my son again," she said. "After that day, I never looked back. I never went back. And I got clean. I went to the shelter on Sussex Avenue. Then I went to the Community Psychiatric Institute, and that's where I got cleaned up."

Fast-forward several years. I was being honored with the Justice Reform award. I walked into the upscale reception hall, and a woman jumped out without warning and embraced me. The force, and surprise, of being enveloped in a bear hug threw me back a few steps. The woman kissed me on the cheek, and somehow her lipstick left a purple smudge on my white cocktail dress. I stood there in distress, looking at the smear, wondering how I would take the stage to accept my award in a stained dress. She said, "Judge, you saved my life."

Looking up, I saw a vaguely familiar face. The woman it belonged to wore a purple dress—matching the lipstick now on my dress—and a radiant smile on her plump, cocoa-brown face. It was Ms. Williams. She had been clean for seven years and was taking medication for her mental illness. She was attending the gala as a prominent and revered member of the organization that was sponsoring the award. She had become a leader in the community, advocating for women's issues and helping political candidates. Her charisma allowed her to approach strangers easily and endear her candidates to them. She had traveled to Washington, DC, to lobby legislators, and had met with two US vice presidents.

Ms. Williams's story offers a remarkable lesson about seeing a person. When she first entered my courtroom, I watched carefully as she spoke. It was not what she said that impacted me but what was behind the words. I could see that she would be receptive to assistance, and that she was a kind person who had lost her way. If I had focused on how she was trying to get over it, I would have missed an opportunity to help her find her way back to a better life.

***

We must also identify what prevents us from seeing people in the first place. One afternoon when the Deuce was packed, I thought I noticed an odd jerking movement out of the corner of my eye. *It could be anything.* I ignored it. *There it goes again. I have to get more sleep.* As cases were resolved and the courtroom slowly emptied, I observed the same motion, but this time I could make it out. It was a dreadlock bouncing on someone's head. I couldn't see the person, but at least I hadn't been hallucinating.

I called the next case. "Darrell Syms! Come on up, sir." There was some rumbling in a row. An ebony-complexioned African American man in his forties stumbled into the aisle. He sluggishly approached counsel's table, dragging his right leg. His head jerked back repeatedly, causing his dreadlocks to flop. Facial twitching caused the right side of his lip to pull back toward his cheekbone. His right arm was immobilized against his chest.

I'm embarrassed to admit that I averted my eyes as he made his way toward the front of the courtroom. Audience members lowered their gaze as he struggled past their rows. It was so painful to watch. When I was a child, my mother instructed me not to stare at the disabled. And to a child, that command translated into *do not look at them*. Unconsciously, I adopted the practice of evading eye contact with disabled people, to avoid causing them discomfort. Unfortunately, I carried that instruction into adulthood.

"Your name for the record, sir," I asked with a lowered gaze.

"Darrell Syms," he grunted from his lopsided mouth. I was told he needed a new court date and an application for a public defender.

Now, this gentleman appeared to suffer from cerebral palsy, but even from my nonmedical background, I knew something else was going on. Maybe he had also suffered a stroke. I approved his application and assigned a second court date.

On his return to court, I once again noticed his severe facial twitching and his head jerking back, causing his long dreadlocks to swing upward as he sat in the audience. I called his case and witnessed a repeat of his painful hobble to counsel's table. On this day, however, I couldn't ignore his discomfort.

"Sir, did you have a stroke?" I inquired as delicately as I could, hoping to offer him an accommodation.

He said, "No, Judge. It's my medication for my mental illness."

I questioned skeptically, "Your medication?"

He said, "Yeah. It makes me like this."

That didn't make sense to me. How could a person see a physician about one thing and leave in worse condition than when they arrived?

Janet Idrogo, the court resource coordinator, who has a degree in forensic mental health counseling, confirmed, "Yes, Judge, those are some of the side effects of the schizophrenia medication. You should see the folks on the hospital floors."

Shock is the only word to describe my feelings at that moment. I asked Mr. Syms if he had spoken to his doctor, and he said, "Yeah, they are trying to fix it."

I asked how long he'd been in that condition. When he said a month, I lost it.

"A month? Did you say a month? You've been suffering like this for a month, and the doctor hasn't gotten it right yet? Unacceptable! I bet if you lived in the suburbs, the doctor would have gotten it right by now." I was practically yelling. "You go back and tell them that they better fix this. The doctor is not a god, and you have a right to receive proper medical care. I'm so tired of these poverty pimps." That term of art refers to individuals and businesses that earn their livelihood exploiting the poor by taking advantage of the monetary benefits, public and private, provided to them—all with no intention of making anyone's life better.

A couple of weeks passed. When I called the next case, a man jumped out of his seat and swaggered confidently to counsel's table. I didn't recognize him. Then I saw it: a slight twitch under his right eye caused his mouth to curve up into a half smile. It was Darrell Syms, who could barely walk a few weeks ago. My jaw dropped. How could it be?

"What happened?" I asked.

He said, "I told the doctor just what you said to tell him."

"Which was what?"

"I told him the judge said don't be giving me no medication that you don't give the white people, and she wants this fixed before I get back to court."

Now, I'm certain that I didn't mention white people. I definitely referred to the disparity in medical treatment based on where people live, revealing socioeconomic status.

He told me that his doctor had immediately lowered his daily medication dosage from 250 mg to 150 mg and reduced the number of injections he received from five per week to two. His girlfriend stood up from the audience and chimed in, "Judge, he started feeling better that evening."

He told me that within days of the changes in dosage, he no longer suffered from the twitches or convulsions. He could walk without dragging his feet. I told him I was proud of him for standing up for himself.

His physical affliction had been man-made. Overmedication was the source of his misery. However, I believe that he felt better the same evening he saw the doctor not merely because of the lowered dosages, but because the act of asserting himself had made him feel like a full man.

He and his girlfriend thanked me. In fact, all I had done was give him words to use to make requests about his health. The new language helped him claim his rights, his dignity, and his humanity. He went back to the doctor and stood up for himself because the judge had shown concern about his condition. The judge had told him he had a right to receive proper treatment and should demand it. Poor, ill-educated, and marginalized people often don't know when it's safe to speak up, or they feel they don't have the right to make basic demands for decent treatment.

Additionally, Mr. Syms made another savvy move. He invoked the name of the judge. Although I didn't tell him to pass on an order from the court to the doctor, he let the doctor know that someone with authority was concerned about his well-being and that consequences might follow if he didn't show improvement. Feeling that he had me in his corner filled him with confidence. He insisted on accountability because someone cared enough about him to insist on it for him.

In the Red Hook Community Justice Center study, court participants indicated that Judge Alex Calabrese, the Brooklyn Community Court judge, "stands up for us."[4] In one of the judge's other roles, that of presiding over housing court, he inspects properties to ensure that housing violations have been addressed by the landlord according to the judge's orders. Unlike the traditional process, which places tenant against landlord—and is perceived by many as David versus Goliath—Judge Calabrese makes the landlord answerable to him. By personally inspecting properties, he holds landlords accountable, ensuring the well-being of the tenant. He uses his position to protect the vulnerable rather than merely ruling in favor the of the powerful. This gives tenants the sense that the judge is genuinely on the side of justice.

In the case of Mr. Syms, a traditional judge caught up in the daily grind of moving cases may have ignored his physical state or neglected to consider his health issues, resulting in a failure by the court to give him the resources he needed to complete rehabilitation for his addiction to illicit drugs. He required extra help to reach the outcome the justice system seeks—that he not reoffend. In his incapacitated state, he did not seem capable of attending drug rehabilitation. Even worse, he may have *increased* his intake of illicit drugs to deal with the side effects of his mental health medication.

In this case, my customary practice initially inhibited my ability to truly see Mr. Syms. It seemed impolite to watch him struggle to walk. It seemed rude to press him for details about his physical impediments. I avoided the glaring issues at first, but not out of malice. I believed that lowering my gaze would be less intrusive. Still, the instinct to avoid acknowledging his struggles prevented me from making a full assessment of him at first. I couldn't help him improve his compliance with court orders if I didn't know what was causing his inability to attend a drug rehabilitation program.

Mr. Syms didn't need my pity. He needed my recognition. Even if his symptoms hadn't resulted from his medication, even if he'd had an incurable condition like cerebral palsy, I still needed to make a proper observation. I needed to ensure that I had a full picture of the individual before me. That required me to correct my automatic reaction to people with physical disabilities. Self-correction, while challenging, is necessary if I want to do better. Justice demands it.

***

Justice requires seeing a person's humanity—the whole person and their circumstances. It requires treating them as more than a problem that needs to be processed or a perpetrator who needs to be punished. To see the individual and their predicament often requires keen observation.

One day, during lunch break, I stood across the street from Newark City Hall, feeling the sun's rays on my skin as they bounced off the building's gold dome. Broad Street, one of the city's busiest throughfares, was bustling as usual. Being out-side helped me unwind. After a court session, I often felt as though I had been in a brawl. The sensation was more physical than you might imagine. There is a bodily manifestation to the emotional toll of the work.

I waited in line on that hot afternoon to order from the food truck with the best fish sandwich in the city. Folks were coming out of city hall, walking back from the federal building and courthouse, when Jason O'Brien walked by. It was hard to ignore the thirty-something, six-foot-five white guy who resembled a Lithuanian basketball player, even on a crowded urban street. I knew him from my courtroom as Mr. Always-Late-to-Court-Ordered-Mandates. I recognized his narrow eyes, weighed down by heavy brown lashes, and his hair in need of a trim. His ruddy, blemished skin revealed years of heroin abuse. His oversized jeans and red T-shirt were dirty, evidence that he'd been sleeping on the street. That day, his entire focus was on his destination. His long strides carried him into the crosswalk. Halfway across the street, he stopped abruptly and turned around. He returned to the curb and headed toward a nearby trash can. He lowered his gangly body to pick up a white piece of debris and throw it into the trash can.

Well, he's not a litterbug. Isn't that a nice thing to learn about him, I thought. Yet that was only the beginning.

He continued on his way. Once again, however, midstride, he stopped in the crosswalk, turned around, and returned to the trash can. He lowered to his knee, picked up an indis-tinguishably tiny item, and threw it into the trash can. *Mr. O'Brien is incredibly committed to this business of keeping Newark clean,* I thought.

I watched in astonishment as he performed the routine another three times. It hit me, *He's not committed, he's obsessed. It's a compulsion.* I realized that this defendant, who was about to be removed from the Newark Community Solutions program and given a jail sentence for noncompliance, suffered from obsessive-compulsive disorder (OCD).

People with OCD have an anxiety disorder characterized by uncontrollable impulses to perform certain routines and acts. In a compulsive ritual driven by an unreasonable fear, Mr. O'Brien could not pass the trash receptacle without throwing little particles of debris into it, again and again. His disorder contributed to his tardiness and his poor attendance in the program. OCD also explained his addiction to heroin. He was self-medicating to control the extreme anxiety he felt, and to subdue, even if only temporarily, his compulsions. In a study of patients who reported for OCD treatment, more than 25 percent also reported a co-occurring substance abuse problem.[5] I reached out to his social worker to discuss my observations.

When Mr. O'Brien returned to court, he stood before me hunched over and defeated. I told him that I had seen him during my lunch break. He lowered his eyes.

"Do you know what I saw?" I asked. He shook his head no.

"I saw you attempting to walk across the street several times before you made it."

A flood of crimson filled his face. "Yeah," he replied with a nervous chuckle.

I continued to write on his file. "Does this happen often?"

"Sometimes I like to clean up things."

"Well, there is cleaning up, and then there is cleaning up, sir." I gently probed. "Does it stop you from getting to where you need to go?"

"Yeah, Judge," he admitted.

"I've spoken to your social worker so that we can focus on this issue. I directed the clinic to give you additional time, a grace period, to come into the building when you're reporting for your appointments," I said.

Weeks later, while I stood in front of the courthouse, I saw Mr. O'Brien again, performing his ritual with the trash can. He had originally entered the criminal justice system due to drug possession charges and quality-of-life violations. Quality-of-life ordinances are created by local governments to make it an offense punishable by fines and/or up to thirty days in jail for sleeping, drinking, or urinating in public, failure to comply with an officer's orders, and the like. I found those particular summonses ironic. Mr. O'Brien probably single-handedly kept the streets as clean as a one-man municipal sanitation department.

When it came to his drug charges, to unearth the fact that he was most likely self-medicating, I had to be willing to see him function in the community, to be outside my courtroom and make observations. To see and be willing to be seen. By no means am I suggesting that judges follow defendants around their neighborhoods to keep an eye on them. My happening to observe folks around the courthouse is different from being nosy. Judges should, however, be willing to step outside the courthouse and to understand the neighborhoods they serve.

It has long been debated whether police officers and judges should be required to live in the communities they serve. People who argue for separation claim that living outside the jurisdiction of employment prevents bias and establishes boundaries in the criminal justice system. There is a fear that judges and police officers may give their neighbors preferential treatment, or that they may be unwilling to make tough calls because of their proximity to the people they exercise authority over. There is also a belief that you attract better talent when individuals can live wherever they wish, without putting restrictions on their families.

Those who support the idea of police residing in the neighborhood they patrol argue that living there will make police more invested in keeping it safe. Additionally, the hope is that such a policy will humanize the residents to the officers. I'm not sure that location alone will fix a broken legal system. I've known plenty of judges and police officers who have worked in the community where they reside, and it has not improved how they treat individuals. Rabbi Joachim Prinz's words at the March on Washington in 1963 are instructive. Before Dr. Martin Luther King Jr. gave his celebrated "I Have a Dream" speech, Rabbi Prinz delivered a speech in which he explained that being a neighbor is about more than geographical proximity. Instead, it is a moral obligation. We have a responsibility to serve people even if we don't share the same zip code. This principle widens the net of our possible neighbors. It creates an obligation to a larger number of people.[6]

Whether a judge or officer lives within the community they serve or nearby, I'd argue that the most important principle to fulfill is their moral obligation: viewing the people they work with as neighbors. We need to be invested in everyone, whether or not they live next door.

I was invested in Mr. O'Brien's case, and I hope I would have observed that something was wrong even if I hadn't witnessed him picking up trash near the courthouse. Being patient and curious enough to find out the underlying causes of his infractions helped me steer him toward a better path.

The willingness to see the whole person is what made me a good neighbor and enabled me to better serve him and my community.

Too often, when we see a person like Mr. O'Brien, we laugh or mock him. We ignore his need for support. Then he makes a poor decision to self-medicate with drugs, gets processed by the system, and ends up before a judge. The judge hammers him because the criminal justice system says to treat everyone like a nail. The underlying causes go completely unaddressed, and he can't climb out of a cycle of repeated arrests.

This is why I approached each individual who came into my courtroom as a whole person, not just a problem to be dealt with or discarded. Too often, professionals in criminal justice have seen their role as punishing the "bad guys," when a defendant's story is usually complicated. Through our court program, Mr. O'Brien received counseling and a referral to mental health services to obtain treatment for both his OCD and drug addiction. He never came through my court again.

***

The celebrated US Supreme Court justice Thurgood Marshall once said, "In recognizing the humanity of our fellow beings, we pay ourselves the highest tribute." When court officials see the humanity in the people who become involved in the justice system, it offers the enormous residual benefit of strengthening an individual's trust in that system. Some benefits can manifest in the most interesting ways.

How long should it take to toast a bagel and slap butter on it? This thought ran through my mind fifteen minutes into my wait at the deli counter across the street from the courthouse. A noisy, increasingly agitated line of customers formed behind me. A woman with shades glided into the deli and recognized another female patron already standing in line. They embraced and started an overly excited exchange.

"Hey, where you going, girl?" asked the lady in sunglasses.

"I have to see Judge Pratt this morning," said her friend.

I cringed and did my best to become invisible at the mention of my name. Damn, I hoped she didn't recognize me and attempt to have an ex parte conversation—an impermissible one-sided communication with the judge—about her case.

"And I didn't get a chance to do my hair, but I hope it's okay," she continued, smoothing her hair back with her hands.

Suddenly, someone approached me from behind and yelled, "All rise!"

Ugh, he blew my cover. I begrudgingly turned around and saw a former colleague from my days working at city hall. I took a deep breath and greeted him.

Astonished, the lady with the court date looked at me in disbelief and said, "Hi, Judge Pratt!"

I said hello and turned around quickly. At this point, my cover was blown, and it was taking too long to get the stupid bagel, so I told the cashier, "Forget the bagel, I'm late."

As I headed to my courtroom, I ran into the lady from the line at the deli. A remnant of the drug crisis that had swept through our community like locusts, she was painfully thin and gaunt. She wore a mint-green skirt suit that was three sizes too big. It had probably fit her at her healthy, sober weight. I smiled because her hair looked fine. Reflecting on the woman's conversation with her friend at the deli, I was struck with the fact that she hadn't said she was going to court or had a case. She said she was coming to see me, Judge Pratt. What was typically a stressful and daunting event had turned into an appointment for which she got dressed up to impress. Why was this? This was something different.

The difference I noticed in the woman's attitude is made plain in Dr. Martin Luther King Jr.'s 1967 speech "What's Your Life's Blueprint?," which he gave at Barratt Junior High School in Philadelphia. He said, "Number one in your life's blueprint should be a deep belief in your own dignity, your own worth, and your own somebodiness. Don't allow anybody to make you feel that you are nobody. Always feel that you count. Always feel that you have worth and always feel that your life has ultimate significance."[7]

Somebodiness is a deep-rooted sense of your worthiness and value. It is a belief that you matter. It's a belief that your life is significant, that someone sees you.

The lady I had overheard in the deli line felt this as she headed to her court date. She knew that the judge saw *her*, not merely her offense. With its traditional conveyor-belt approach to dispensing justice, our criminal justice system usually robs court litigants of their sense of worth. It robs them of the inner resolve that tells them, shows them, and reminds them that they matter. But for this woman, her court dates became times for checking in with the judge. The judge was helping her get better by making her do things she wouldn't do on her own. Things she didn't know she *could* do, like show up on time. The idea is to sow the seeds of hope with every court appearance. Convincing this woman that she was capable was accomplished in part by the judge's noticing her and holding her accountable to her progress. This allowed her to enter the courtroom with a sense of hope. Her mandated court dates metamorphosed into welcome appointments with someone who cared about her and who would cheer her on. Getting dressed up for her court date to enter a place where she knew she would be seen also helped her find and maintain her own dignity.

By seeing and noticing people, I can dispel the notion that the judge, prosecutor, and police are in cahoots and are working against them. People feel lost in our system for good reason—it's not set up for the layperson to understand or navigate easily. They distrust the courts from the beginning because of their initial contact. Whatever hostility they experienced with law enforcement or on a previous visit to court, they bring that hostility back on their next court date. Unfortunately, this attitude can make their appearance in court go south. It doesn't help if they insult the prosecutor or are angry with their own attorney. I can also assure you that things won't go well if they direct that hostility toward the judge.

***

Justice also requires that you see, understand, and correct your missteps as you try to do what's right. For me, this was the situation in Angela Andujar's case.

One day, I saw a little boy dressed in a navy-blue shorts set scamper in, struggling to keep up with Ms. Andujar as she strutted into the courtroom. *Could this be her kid?* I wondered as I watched the boy—he was perhaps five or six years old—fly his toy car through the air. In all her previous appearances, among all the excuses she had concocted to explain why she missed her court-ordered mandates and court appearances, she had never mentioned having a child.

I shrugged it off. Today she would be finished with the Newark Community Solutions program. Participants often brought their mothers, family members, or other loved ones to witness them receive accolades for completion. Maybe that's why she had brought her son.

She stood before me with her blond ponytail pulled tightly back, exposing dark brown roots and large hoop earrings. As she attempted to pull off her J.Lo look, she rolled her eyes, glanced at the ceiling, and sucked her teeth as if I were the bus driver making her late to work. Her behavior didn't immediately surprise me as she always presented with a funky attitude—one that was completely impenetrable. However, I did find it unusual for someone who should be finishing a court-mandated program. Especially since I had read her the riot act during her last court appearance. That had been her fourth, and final, opportunity to get in compliance or receive the suspended jail sentence she had agreed to when she originally pled guilty. In no uncertain terms, I had told her that if she missed any more of her court-ordered requirements, I would remove her from the program and require her to serve her jail sentence. It had been her last opportunity to comply.

Imagine my surprise as I heard for the fifth time that this young woman had failed to show up to her community service appointments or her counseling sessions. I held my head in my hands and said to myself, *No. Not the twenty-year-old high school dropout with prior heroin possession convictions. Not the young woman gullible enough to hold drugs for the male gang members and then take the heat and plead guilty. She couldn't have missed her days again.*

I looked up quizzically at Ms. Andujar. We know that the prisons are full of people without high school diplomas. With this behavior she was effectively reserving her "cot with three hots" (hot meals) in the Edna Mahan Correctional Facility for Women, New Jersey's only women's prison.

She stood before me defiantly, arms crossed, eyebrow raised, reddish-pink lips pursed. Her brown eyes did not flinch. At that moment, I realized she had brought her child to court to avoid going to jail. She thought she'd manipulate me, pull on my sympathy, and force me to be lenient even when I had already told her the consequences of noncompliance. Rather than actually comply, she thought she'd avoid jail time, and I'd waive her sentence just because I'd feel bad following through when her son was watching.

I. Lost. It! I went from zero to sixty in five seconds.

"How dare you! How dare you bring your child here when you know you are going to jail! How dare you!" I screamed as I felt my blood rise. "You know the consequences you're facing! Do you think having your child here today is going to prevent me from sending you to jail? Not at all! The law tells me to call child services. I've seen some low things in this court; this is the lowest!"

I directed the officer to escort Ms. Andujar to the holding cell. As the officer approached her, I heard a loud shriek—a sound an animal might make when caught in a metal hunting trap. I had never heard anything so painful. It was her son. He stopped racing his car on the counsel's table and wrapped his arms around his mother. He screamed, "No, don't take my mommy! Don't take my mommy!"

My heart dropped to my feet. The prosecutor's eyes welled up with tears. Audience members shook their heads and looked down. The police officer's legs became rooted like tree trunks on the courtroom floor. Ms. Andujar pulled her son closer, as though he could protect her from the results of her behavior.

The officer, uncertain as to what to do, looked at me for guidance. No one was going to rip this child from his mother's embrace. I had to make a decision quickly. If I let her go, she would continue to use her son as a prop for the next visit to court. I decided that today, she had to face her consequences.

I instructed the officer to take them into the room that separated the courtroom from the holding cell. From there, Ms. Andujar could call someone to retrieve her child before she was sent to the cellblock. Unbeknownst to us, she had come to court with a friend who was waiting in the hallway.

I called a recess and went to my office and cried uncontrollably. That child had been traumatized as a part of my process. His trust of the court system, even his ability to trust people in authority, might never be the same. Perhaps all he understood was that the judge yelled at his mother for bringing him to court. I worried that he somehow thought he was to blame for his mother's trouble. He would not understand the peril she had put him in by bringing him to court on a day she was facing jail.

The friend retrieved the child and waited until Ms. Andujar's father arrived. The father told the police officer that he refused to pay bail because it was time that his daughter became responsible. "Today, she is going to learn her lesson," he said.

He said that he and his wife were raising the boy, whom Ms. Andujar never bothered to watch. They were shocked that on this particular day she had volunteered to take the child out with her.

After Ms. Andujar had spent a few days in jail and received a stern reprimand from me, I decided that I would release her for the time she'd served and vacate her fines. I explained, "What you've done to your child is greater punishment than I could ever give you. You decided to use him as a shield against the consequences you had to answer for in this court. And I hope that you spend the rest of your life making it up to him."

She replied, "I had a lot of time to think in here. The women gave me a lot of advice."

Unfortunately, I had violated my own rule. It's the rule that says when I feel the tidal wave of heat rise through my body, I need to abruptly disengage, lower my gaze from whoever is causing the frustration, and breathe. Instead, I leaned into that tide and rode it. My frustration blinded me from the perspective of the child before me. I had a responsibility to him too. Ironically, my anger with Ms. Andujar for what I saw as mistreatment of her son made me complicit in the very trauma I had warned her about. While I don't regret holding her accountable, I do regret losing my temper and scaring her son.

The incident turned into fodder for my naysayers when I came up for future promotions. One of my colleagues anonymously sent a recording of the exchange to individuals in decision-making positions. They attached a false label: "Judge Pratt Sends a Child to Jail."

The English jurist William Blackstone famously proposed, "Better that ten guilty persons escape, than that one innocent suffer." This doctrine instructs that we should err on the side of protecting innocent people. Rather than hiding my failure to safeguard that young boy, I'm telling you this story because it is important to understand that judges are human beings. In some cases, our mistakes can result in a miscarriage of justice and negatively impact others.

Months later, after finishing all my cases one day, I noticed two people remaining in the audience. I assumed they were waiting on behalf of a defendant who'd been arrested the night before and was in police custody. The young woman pulled her scarf over her face and turned up her collar. I looked at her suspiciously. She nervously avoided my gaze.

Something in those eyes looked familiar. I asked, "Ma'am, are you waiting for someone in custody?"

She looked up and mumbled yes through her scarf. It was Ms. Andujar.

"Stop trying to hide, ma'am. I already recognized you. You're the young woman with the little boy. Come on up here and tell me what is going on with you." She seemed surprised. "What are you doing here?"

"Judge, I'm just here to see what's going on with my son's godfather," she explained.

"What have you been up to, ma'am?"

"Judge, I don't even get into arguments on the streets anymore. I just walk away because I'm not trying to come back here and see you," she said. "I have a job at the supermarket. I start school in January to get my GED. My family thanks you. I thank you. I'm not going to jail again."

"Remember that your son comes first," I reminded her. She nodded and said she was spending more time with him.

In retrospect, if I had to do it all over again, she would still have gone to jail. Would I have handled the situation differently? Of course. I would have re-called her case. I would have made her sit down in the audience and have her call someone to retrieve the child before I sent her to the cellblock. The grandparents would have been able to come to the courthouse and take their grandson. If no one were available to retrieve the boy, I would be responsible for calling child protective services. The agency would have sent a representative to the courtroom to take the child. If no one was available to take possession of him, he would have been placed in the foster care system. He would never have experienced that traumatic scene. I have learned to count to twenty because counting to ten isn't nearly enough.

Did I obtain the result I wanted for Ms. Andujar? Yes. I wanted her to change her life and get on the right path. I wanted her to stay away from the gang members who turned her into a drug mule. I wanted her to stay out of the women's prison. I still feel a tightening in my stomach when I think about what happened. I learned not to lose sight of the larger consequences of my actions just because I'm narrowly focused on the person before me.

I told Ms. Andujar I was proud of her. She told me she was proud of herself.

Years later, I saw her in the courthouse outside the traffic court. She said, "I just have a traffic ticket, Judge." It was truly a relief.

* * *

Improving your perception is not an easy undertaking. To do so, I recommend that you solicit help from others. I enlist my staff to help me improve my ability to see the things around me I would otherwise overlook. For years I ended court sessions by asking them, "Okay, what did I miss?"

My query would be met with comments such as, "Judge, the boyfriend was intimidating her." "The gentleman was talking to himself all day." "The young man wanted to tell you something else."

Too often, the criminal justice system is overly focused on going after the bad guy. This causes us to miss opportunities to achieve better outcomes. We must look, see, and perceive so that we can grasp the entire incident behind why someone is in the system. People are more than the events that bring them to court. If we want them to stay out of the system, we need to be willing to unearth root causes, which requires curiosity and a keen eye that sees that which is not obvious.

According to a study by the National Judicial College, one of the common mistakes that new judges make is allowing themselves to become afflicted by Black Robe Disease or Black Robe Syndrome. This ailment causes the judge to inflate their sense of self-importance, to believe they have infallible judgment, and to focus on their own status. The recurring symptoms can be meanness, a lack of empathy, and a tendency to believe they wear a cape and not a robe. They are prevented from using sound judgment and seeing the full humanity of the individual before them.[8]

Instead, when judges focus our attention on things that appear unusual, out of the ordinary, or uncommon, we can help the system do a better job of observing and deciphering the big-picture situation instead of immediately jumping into the penalty phase. There are considerable factors that impede one's ability to see. We must identify and overcome those influences. Our willingness to truly see people who come into contact with the justice system is key to transforming it into an institution that assists people in correcting their behavior. Most importantly, we must see their full humanity.

I once worked with a court administrator who referred to certain defendants as "regulars." She said it with disdain, often rolling her eyes. I was struck that she said it as if they came to court voluntarily, like they were going to the neighborhood bar. We talked about why she felt that way, and I urged her to pay more attention to what was going on behind the low-level offenses that triggered recidivism. As she began to listen closely to the defendants' stories, she started to fill in the blanks about them and to see them as full humans, not just multiple tickets and dispositions she was required to put into the computer system.

From the perspective of this employee, and many others, these folks overwhelmed the system and inundated her workload. She saw them at their worst, through the lens of a system that was not well equipped to turn them around. Understanding their backstory opened her sight so she could see beneath the surface of their actions.

Throughout this chapter, we've examined the power of seeing people beyond the circumstances that bring them to court. The power arises from widening our vision to amplify dignity in our interpersonal interactions. Our perceptions include our biases and our understanding of the world. To overcome those prejudices, we must create a model, a process, that routinely challenges us to see beyond them so we can view the entirety of our fellow human beings. When we attempt to uncover what is missing or unobvious, we can overcome our preconceived notions about people and their actions and create better outcomes. This expanded vision also allows us to have a greater impact in reducing inequities in our justice system for the most vulnerable.

Chapter 4

POVERTY IS NOT A CRIME

*Addressing poverty is not a gesture of charity. It is
an act of justice. It is the protection of a fundamental
human right, the right to dignity and a decent life.
While poverty persists, there is no true freedom.*
—NELSON MANDELA

I knocked on the door before I made my entrance. Officer Mickey Carillo announced, "All rise. This is Part Two Criminal Court, the Honorable Judge Victoria Pratt presiding." I stepped onto the bench and took my seat. I saw an assembly of substantially impoverished, overwhelmingly addicted Black and Brown people, many with mental illness, and all suffering from uninterrupted trauma. Most people believe that court resembles the procedural police and courtroom shows, like the *Law and Order* franchise. That, however, is Hollywood. The scene before me was of everyday, abandoned America. These folks were facing direct and collateral consequences based on the decisions that would be made in court that day. Incarceration, eviction, loss of government benefits, loss of employment, suspension of a driver's license, and insur-mountable debt were just a few of the catastrophic events that could result from a court case, upending a person's life when they already live in poverty.

"What is that putrid smell?" I gagged as police officers brought the people held in custody of the city jail into the courtroom, chained to one another. My nose involuntarily restricted my breathing to object to the entrance of the suf-focating odor through my nostrils. I held my breath until I was forced to take in a gulp of rancid air. My saliva glands immediately went to work to expel the burning taste from my mouth. The court administrator sprayed Lysol to cover the odor. No luck. A police officer burned incense and hung it on the window frame to cut through the foulness. It didn't work. As the daughter of a garbageman, I've smelled some unpleasant odors. The stench that day was so overpowering that I began to feel ill.

"What is it?" I demanded.

Officer Carillo approached the bench and whispered, "It's the guy on the end, Judge. His foot has gangrene."

Rotting flesh. The smell of death on a living body. It's the stench of poverty.

"There but for the grace of God go I," I mumbled under my breath, grateful that I had been spared his condition.

The afflicted person was a homeless man from Newark Penn Station, filthy, sick, and despondent. He was in custody for a quality-of-life violation. The arresting officer had treated him like a piece of tainted meat. He had thrown the man into the back of his police cruiser, driven him to the courthouse, and dumped him in the city jail. What would possess a police officer to bring this suffering soul to the courthouse? Wouldn't a trip to the hospital have been more feasible? More humane? How could the officer not see this person's humanity? What gives us, members of the criminal justice system, the right to shut our eyes to the suffering that's directly in front of us? This man was not a threat.

I admonished the court police officers for not telling me about his condition earlier. We could have already handled his case and sent him to the hospital.

The arresting officer should have handled the situation differently. He should have taken this gentleman and his diseased foot to a physician who could offer medication, not a judge wielding a gavel. Instead, the officer checked his records and found that the man had an open bench warrant. He had been previously charged with sleeping in public—a violation of the quality-of-life summons. But when you are homeless, public spaces become your only possible residences. The charging officer knew that the man wouldn't make it to court on his own due to his physical and mental state. So he carted his infirm body through the city because of the minor infraction.

I wanted to help him, but I couldn't focus. The pungent odor emanating from his foot made it difficult to breathe. I dismissed his ticket for the time served in the city jail. I had the court administrator check the computer system to ensure he had no other tickets pending. Unfortunately, in a court system as large as Newark's, an individual can have numerous unresolved quality-of-life tickets, as well as other bench warrants for unpaid fines. Pulling all the files together would help prevent the defendant from being rearrested and held in custody, having to appear before a judge multiple times.

The officers arranged to have the defendant taken to the hospital. The Newark Community Solutions representative provided him with information so he could return to the clinic after his hospital stay and get connected to services.

He was a harmless person that the criminal justice system punished because of his lack of housing and other resources. That's how the system deals with poverty and the people engulfed by it. The Population Research Institute asserts, "Poverty is like darkness; it's not a thing. It's the lack of a thing."[1] I agree. Poverty is about being in a state of scarcity. Poor people lack the essentials necessary to meet their basic needs—the social, economic, educational, and political resources that most of us take for granted. In a vicious cycle, the lack hinders their ability to acquire these resources, not only creating barriers to their survival, but derailing their ability to live full, safe, and productive lives.

Poor people lack access to health care. Many of them also lack a clear understanding of their health, both physical and mental. They usually inhabit areas plagued by violence. Poverty causes them to live without assured shelter, with food insecurity, and with inadequate education. Then the justice system punishes them for the lack by making it illegal to be without those resources.

The poverty and the mental state of the homeless man who appeared in court that day are what drove his contact with the criminal justice system. If that suffering individual didn't deserve sympathy, then who does? The corrosively punitive practices of law enforcement and our courts eat away at a community's very soul. They require us to ignore people's humanity and to forfeit ours as well. That man's situation demanded empathy. In fact, I'm asking for more than sympathy. I'm asking for benevolence. By criminalizing the acts that poverty-stricken people are forced to take, we make poverty appear as something it's not: sinister and evil.

We should think of the criminal justice system as a ship. We, the practitioners, cannot merely be travelers on the journey. We must see ourselves as the crew doing the daily work.

Many folks trapped in the unyielding cycle of poverty are grinding and scraping to get by—living paycheck to paycheck, if they even have employment—and then they have an encounter with law enforcement. Maybe their car's headlight is out, and they get stopped by a police officer. Perhaps they had to choose between buying groceries and paying other bills, like the woman with young children who came through my court after receiving a ticket for driving without insurance. She agreed to plead guilty to the $1,000 fine and the one-year license suspension, even though by the time her case had been called her next paycheck had arrived and she had obtained car insurance.

Do I think she'll continue driving, even with a suspended license? Of course. She will need to drive to work and take her four children to school. Will she pay the $1,000 fine? Probably not. It's damn near impossible to get water from a rock. If she has an unpaid fine, she'll be facing a jail sentence with the next traffic ticket she receives.

In our courts, the ravages of poverty are hidden in plain sight. We just choose to ignore them. I deplore the criminal justice system's tendency to throw its hands up and claim that we aren't equipped to handle social issues. That assertion is not true.

In fact, as stewards of justice we don't have the luxury of disregarding the social problems of those overcrowding our courts, jails, and prisons. In her address to newly admitted members of the Washington State Bar, Justice Mary E. Fairhurst expounded on this notion:

> The next step is to commit ourselves to be stewards of justice. How does one be a steward of justice? First, if you see justice is not being achieved, do something about it. When the public repeatedly sees the justice system fail, the people's confidence in the law will soon decline. If you see the system fail, propose changes in the laws or changes in the rules. You have the skills, training, and ability to make a difference, to have an impact. As good stewards of justice, we must be driven to make the law work in the real world. As Justice Stephen Breyer has said, "The law should provide real answers, to help real people, with real problems."[2]

As stewards or agents of justice, we cannot turn a blind eye to the effects of poverty on the individuals who come through our justice system. Instead, we need to shine a light on its daily, far-reaching ramifications. Poverty creates an inescapable, never-ending flow of people into our justice system. In particular, the lack of access to a proper education not only keeps people trapped in poverty, but too often it traps them in a cycle of arrests that they can never escape.

The story of Candance Chanel illustrates this point. Her thick, stiff, jet-black dreadlocks lay disheveled on the top of her head. She whipped her head in an upward motion to move the strays that attempted to land on her face. Her delicate features contrasted with the street gear that weighed down her slight frame—a man's outdoor vest, oversized shirt, sagging jeans, and the requisite camel-colored, untied Timberland boots. She dressed like her colleagues, the young guys who sold drugs on neighborhood street corners. When she spoke, she revealed a missing front tooth. It reminded me that dental work is costly, and she was one of many who came before me who had not had any.

The resource coordinator's report revealed that Ms. Chanel was noncompliant with her court-ordered mandates. She arrived late for her appointments or not at all. Unable to get her to talk to me about what was going on, I decided to assign her an essay, "Why I Need to Show Up on Time." The assignment caused her entire demeanor to change. She protested, and I sent her on her way.

The prosecutor subsequently asked to approach the bench. "Judge," she whispered, "Candance stopped me in the hallway. She meant no disrespect. She can't write the essay because she can't read or write."

Damn. A high school dropout, Ms. Chanel had somehow managed to get to the age of twenty-five without learning to read or write. Who else would offer her employment but your friendly neighborhood drug dealer? Ms. Chanel, however, had another problem. She was a terrible drug dealer. She had no talent for it. She regularly got arrested, as evidenced by her cases at both the municipal and state-level courts. She had already spent time in both the county jail and the women's prison. Her lack of literacy made her unemployable, and she was a prime candidate for a life spent cycling in and out of prison.

Sadly, Ms. Chanel's case was not unique. The link between educational failure and incarceration is clear—our prisons are full of people who haven't graduated from high school. According to data from the National Former Prisoner Survey, formerly incarcerated people are twice as likely as the general population to have no high school diploma.[3]

Poverty creates a barrier to quality education. It had deprived Ms. Chanel, who suffered a learning disability, the fundamental right to an education. She barely completed the court program. It was difficult to tell if that was because she was unmotivated or because she had cognitive issues. Ultimately, she landed in the women's correctional facility for violating the terms of her superior court probation.

I thought of Ms. Chanel when I was later introduced to what I came to call the "Montgomery Street School defense." After noticing the public defender arguing with a client as I was arraigning him, I asked, "Counselor, is there something you'd like to add?" To myself, I wondered, *Didn't they have a conversation before I got to his client's case?*

"No, Judge." He shook his head and waved his hand in exasperation.

His client nudged him with his elbow and whispered loudly, "Tell her, tell her."

The public defender rolled his eyes and relented. "He wanted me to tell you he went to Montgomery Street School, Judge," he said, shrugging his shoulders because he couldn't understand why that would be important. Neither did I.

No sooner had he said it than people began to snicker. Another judge, Bahir Kamil, my mentor, happened to be in the courtroom that day. A native Newarker and highly regarded, he approached the bench and explained that, historically, students with learning disabilities attended Montgomery Street School. In the 1960s and 1970s, it had been identified as a school for remedial learning and disciplinary action. Attending it made students the objects of ridicule. These days, I believe we would call sending kids there the warehousing of students with cognitive issues.

The Montgomery Street School defense essentially said, "Something is wrong with me; I can't think well. Please show me mercy." No one expected anything from the students who attended that school. Therefore, like many students who have learning disabilities and disciplinary problems, no one bothered to cultivate them into self-sufficient, productive members of society. Students attending Montgomery Street School wore a badge of dishonor that carried a stigma many of them internalized. They were ill equipped to lead constructive lives. Their condition also made them more vulnerable to the pressures of drug use. Of course many of them would end up in the criminal justice system.

In the years that followed, I heard a version of the Montgomery Street School defense from multiple defendants. Many of the school's former students were hapless drug addicts who cycled repeatedly through the courts. What if they had been mainstreamed into regular schools and had received an appropriate education, with tutoring, therapy, and support, like their remedial counterparts in the suburbs? Would that have provided the exit ramp they needed to thrive? But there are few off-ramps from poverty, and the highway leads straight to jail or prison. Newark's underresourced school system simply wasn't able to provide all its students with the kind of education they needed to succeed in twenty-first-century America. To recognize this reality, you have to be able to see through the fog of poverty, which hovers over nearly everything that happens in the criminal justice system.

***

The fog of poverty was most definitely a factor in the police shooting and killing of the unarmed African American teenager Michael Brown in Ferguson, Missouri, which triggered protests and riots across the country. The incident prompted the US Department of Justice (DOJ) to investigate the Ferguson Police Department. The investigation found that the police committed various unlawful practices and constitutional violations, primarily against Ferguson's Black residents. Equally important, the report pulled the covers back on what was occurring in the Ferguson Municipal Court and in municipal courts across the country.[4] The significance of this discovery is that it laid bare our courts' unreasonable financial impositions. Court was effectively being used as a vehicle for transferring wealth from poor people to the local government. The process did not feel like the operation of an impartial system devoted to seeking justice.

Here's how it worked: Defendants were brought to court for any of a host of violations, many of which resulted in the imposition of fees and fines. Whether a defendant could pay or not was practically immaterial. When a defendant failed to meet the requirements, the court simply responded with added fees—and arrest warrants. The arrest warrants were used almost exclusively to compel payment through the threat of incarceration. As a result, minor violations could result in multiple arrests and fees that vastly exceeded the original ticket's cost. The Ferguson Police Department was being used in large part as a collection agency for the municipal court. The conclusion reached by the DOJ investigation was stark: the push for revenue undermined the court's role. Unfortunately, this is how it works across the country.

The report detailed the city's violations of its Black residents' First, Fourth, and Fourteenth Amendment rights. Additionally, the investigation found evidence that officers' violations of Black residents' rights were driven by prejudice and racial bias. And it uncovered egregious violations motivated by the Ferguson City Council's urging for substantial annual increases in the municipal court's revenue. In the words of the report:

- The court's focus on revenue impaired the court's position as a fair and impartial judicial body.

- Ferguson's harmful law enforcement practices in recent years were the result of the court's excessive, customary use of arrest warrants to collect outstanding monies and for failing to appear in court.

- Ferguson's bond practices created an undue hardship for those detained and seeking release from the Ferguson City Jail.[5]

The court system's primary goal was maximizing revenue at the expense of poorer residents, as opposed to administering justice and protecting rights. The criminal justice system at the municipal court level was essentially an exchange of wealth from the poor to the government. And that is because the state receives the vast majority of funds that the town or city collects. The court demands its remuneration, and the defendant is required to figure out how to pay it. The process keeps defendants in a state of debt—and sacrifices their liberty. It extracts money from folks who we know can't pay, and then exacts punishment for nonpayment. Believe it or not, this is how the system is set up to work. These individuals should be offered community service if they are unable to pay, but that option is often not considered.

I wish I could say that such practices are exclusive to Ferguson, but they are not. While attending a function, I once heard a judge introduce himself to a chief judge from another jurisdiction by saying, "Hello. I'm Judge X from Y, and I made my town $4 million last year." My stomach turned. Was he a used car salesman or a judge? Yet I understood what he was doing. He wanted to impress the chief judge with his extraordinary ability to squeeze money out of people, and he wanted that chief judge to give him per diem work in his town. (In per diem work, a judge is hired to work for a daily fee in a jurisdiction outside his or her originating court.) That judge knew the game. It was not about justice. The more money he could make for a jurisdiction, the more money he earned for himself by getting awarded more per diem work.

When I first became a judge, before I began the difficult work in Newark of dramatically expanding sentencing options, I often felt like a fool participating in the masquerade called "revising time payments." The charade would go like this: I'd address the drug-sick addict leaning against counsel's table. "Sir, when are you gonna be able to pay this money? You owe close to $2,000 here."

"Yeah, yeah, yeah, Judge," he'd stammer while feigning a calculation of his nonexistent funds. "I'ma pay you next month." The simple ruse would begin.

"How are you going to pay, sir?"

"When I get my check," he'd assure me. "When I get my check, I'ma pay you $100 a month."

"One hundred dollars a month?" He could have said $500 to make it more dramatic.

"Yeah, Judge." He'd begin to fidget. All this questioning was holding up his next hit.

"Okay, sir. I'm going to revise the time payment, and you can start making your $100 payment next month. But please don't miss your payment because a bench warrant will issue for your arrest."

The game was far from over. I'd subsequently reduce the amount to $50 or $25 because the original amount looked so ridiculous in my handwriting when it came back to me on rearrest. I'd write the agreement on the court's files as the previous judges had done before me. These payments were often revised and extended numerous times over several years. It was a sham. It made me feel dirty. I didn't go to law school to be a collection agent. And judges are still required to do it. The process of revising time payments in these situations makes judges' actions inconsistent with their pledge to administer justice. We know they will lead to inevitable jail sentences.

Discretionary fines for misdemeanor offenses in New Jersey can be upwards of $1,000. Each conviction carries a mandatory $75 fee for the Safe Neighborhood Street Fund and $50 for the Violent Crime Compensation Board. Not to mention the $33 in court costs for processing the matter. These charges can also carry up to 180 days in jail. Fines for violating a city ordinance—typically quality-of-life citations—can be upwards of $500 plus $33 in court costs, and can include up to 30 days in jail.

On a drug possession or drug paraphernalia charge, the defendant must pay fines, mandatory fees, court costs, and an

additional $500 to New Jersey's Drug Education Demand Re-
duction Fund. One incident can carry several counts, as it is often the practice of law enforcement and the prosecutor's office
to throw in everything under the sun. Therefore, a single arrest
may result in the imposition of fines, mandatory fees, and court
costs multiple times over.

A judge's arms are tied if a defendant agrees to plead guilty
to the offenses. While the judge may reduce the fines and the
court costs, there remains the issue of mandatory fees. Fortunately, New Jersey legislators passed a law that allows a judge to
vacate—that is, remove—those fees. Before this, being unable
to vacate the mandatory fines resulted in multiple arrests for
failing to pay mandatory fees in cases in which the defendant
may have already served time in jail. People who couldn't afford
to pay would continue to be held in custody for the mandatory
fines and fees they still owed. Although the double jeopardy
clause of the Fifth Amendment of the US Constitution prevents individuals from being tried a second time after acquittal
or conviction, protecting them from multiple punishments, it
appears to do nothing to protect poverty-stricken people who
commit low-level offenses.

Another often unseen, or merely ignored, manner in which
our justice system ensnares people who are poor, working class,
and even middle class is through the proliferation of parking
tickets and the subsequent towing of vehicles. These cases
come to my attention due to the numerous parking summonses
I have had to dismiss because they were issued while the car
was legally parked. For example, on Broad Street in Newark,
it is illegal to have your vehicle parked on a certain side of
the street from Monday to Friday after 4:00 p.m. Frequently
drivers would contest tickets they received for that particular

violation because the police officer issued the ticket at 3:57 p.m., 3:58 p.m., or 3:59 p.m., as written on the ticket by the officer. Even if the vehicle was unlawfully parked there at or after 4:00 p.m., the real issue becomes the towing charges. Once the car is hooked to the tow truck, the individual is charged $185 by the towing company.

Many tow services charge an unhooking fee if the owner arrives before they have physically moved the vehicle. This fee may be over $100, and it has to be paid on the spot by the driver. Once the car arrives at the impound lot, however, an additional fee is assessed. Even if the vehicle owner arrives within five minutes of the tow company moving their vehicle to the impound lot, the owner is charged. The owner has already amassed approximately $200 that must be paid to retrieve the car, and then a storage fee is assessed for every day the vehicle stays at the lot. The accumulating sums make it very difficult for people of limited financial means to get their car out of the impound. The longer it takes them to pay the necessary fees to regain possession of their car, the more money they owe. In many instances, the combined costs quickly exceed the value of the vehicle. At some point, the owner of the towing company becomes the owner of the vehicle, which they eventually sell at an auction. The original owner didn't abandon the vehicle; rather, the egregious accumulating fees made it impossible for them to recover possession of it.

How is it fair that a ticket worth $45 can cause the disposition of ownership of someone's means of transportation, especially if that person cannot raise the funds to free their car from the claws of the towing industry? This process looks like theft—and feels like it to the vehicle owner. And the worst part is that our justice system triggers it. Once again, the justice system robs people of their dignity by setting the wheels in motion, starting with the officer who calls the towing company.

Think about it. The justice system appears to be in cahoots with the towing service. The dispossessed person's life is totally disrupted and probably irreparably harmed. They can no longer use their car to get to work, to transport their children to school, or to take family members to the doctor. They can no longer do the things most of us take for granted. And there is no recourse for them because they are poor and lack disposable income.

Even worse was when the vehicle owner would return to court to ask me how to help them get their car back after they'd paid their parking ticket. I had to tell them I was not connected to that part of the process, and there was nothing I could do for them. This seems ridiculous. For the person on the receiving end of the disaster, it feels like a violation of the Eighth Amendment—the one prohibiting cruel and unusual punishment—just for being poor or broke, or waking up too late, or not moving their car in time.

By no means am I letting legislators off the hook who draft and proliferate these rules and regulations. Such laws hurt the most vulnerable of the people they are sworn to serve. For the person living in poverty, it is another blow that sets them back and keeps them from reaching the American dream.

*＊＊

Women are another unseen casualty of the war against the poor that is waged by our criminal justice system. Historically, when men are removed from their communities, women have been left to bear the family's financial burdens. Unfortunately, for the mostly Black and Latina women shouldering the burden of having a loved one embroiled in the criminal justice system, working and finding ways to make ends meet have never been optional. And when their loved one returns with a criminal conviction or serves time, according to a recent report from the Brennan Center for Justice, the average lost earnings potential for those individuals over their lifetimes amounts to $372 billion nationwide. The financial implications for African Americans and Latinos are especially staggering.[6]

When a family is in crisis, women's finances suffer. That's because it is the mothers, wives, girlfriends, grandmothers, aunts, daughters, and nieces who inequitably shoulder the costs of the justice system. They post bails, pay fines, put money in commissaries, accept collect calls with prohibitive surcharges from jail, and pay to travel for prison visits.

Women constantly filled the court benches in the courtroom where I served waiting to see people in custody. They took time off their jobs to be there. Many of them wore their work uniforms; they were hourly wage employees, living paycheck to paycheck. They said they worried about whether they would have enough money to cover bail, and how being in court and not at work jeopardized their jobs.

One woman who came to court had to decide whether to post her boyfriend's bail or pay the rent—not unusual. She decided to post bail to prevent him from going to the county jail. A week or so later, she returned to court to see me. "Judge," she explained, "I posted bail for him last week. I need my money back so I can pay my rent."

"Ma'am, bail is to ensure that the defendant returns to court to respond to the proceedings. The court holds the bail for the duration of the case, which can take months," I told her.

"But Judge, I didn't know that. I've got to pay my rent!" she replied in desperation.

I usually released the bail out of compassion, but sometimes the scenario played out differently. Sometimes I'd have to tell the girlfriend, sister, or mother of a defendant, "Ma'am, your bail is forfeited because the defendant did not come to court on his court date. That means the court keeps the bail. You shouldn't post bail for someone if you can't ensure they return to court." I put it in plain words. This realization was followed by tears.

"How am I going to make my bills? Why does the court get to keep my money? I haven't done anything wrong."

The organizations Forward Together, Ella Baker Center for Human Rights, and Research Action Design summarized the findings of a study undertaken by twenty national groups in a report titled *Who Pays? The True Cost of Incarceration on Families*. They found that:

- 83 percent of the individuals responsible for paying fees and costs related to arrest through conviction were women.

- 38 percent of those surveyed had an annual income of less than $15,000, and on average amassed $13,607 in attorney and case-related fees.

- 34 percent of those surveyed went into debt, incurring expenses through phone calls and visits to remain connected to incarcerated loved ones.

- Two in five were subsequently denied housing, faced eviction, or became ineligible for public housing once their incarcerated loved one returned home.

- 65 percent of families surveyed that had an incarcerated loved one could not meet their basic needs.

• 49 percent of families surveyed that had an incarcerated loved one found it difficult to meet their basic food needs.[7]

Not only are the people who offend punished, but so are the women in their lives and their entire families. It's as if the system punishes loved ones for caring for a person and wanting to support them through their involvement with the criminal justice system.

The report sheds additional light on how the collateral impact of that system mostly affects women and, more specifically, communities of color. Almost one in four women of color is related to someone who's incarcerated; for Black women that figure is two out of five. These facts highlight the racial injustice steeped into our system, and they challenge the belief that the offender is the only one impacted by court-imposed punishment. Again, the financial costs of incarceration unfairly affect women of color and their families, potentially leading to emotional problems, including trauma.

Transgender and gender nonconforming people also deal with the challenges of inequality in the criminal justice system. Jessica Tavares, an Afro-Latina transgender woman, walked through the world with her fists clenched because she had been the recipient of so many blows, literally and figuratively. She managed to eke out a marginal existence as a prostitute, as did the majority of transgender women I encountered in court. They were regularly brought in due to police raids of the prostitution stroll. Who hires transgender women in poor communities? Johns, who are rarely arrested. Ms. Tavares, like her colleagues who were also Black, subjected herself to the dangers of the sex trade for her livelihood.

The reality of this violence came to bear later, in Ms. Tavares's missed court appearance. Her boyfriend approached the counsel's table with a police report and photos as evidence that she had been hospitalized after a robbery that resulted in her receiving close to a hundred stitches in her head. The photograph depicted a brutalized Ms. Tavares with a swollen-shut eye and blood and bruises all over her face. The dark, thick stiches ran from one side of her head to the other, reminiscent of Frankenstein's creature. A john was responsible.

When she eventually returned to court, she was still attempting to recuperate her ability to speak. Transgender women who toil in the sex trade typically do so to earn money to purchase hormones under the table and to obtain body augmentations. These clandestine procedures, often performed at "pump parties" at hotels by unlicensed practitioners, aid in their transition, since sex-reassignment surgery is not within their reach financially. While they are cheaper, the clandestine procedures put them at substantial risk of death.

Ms. Tavares, while struggling for acceptance and establishing her gender identity, had battled a lifetime of untreated trauma and neglected bipolar disorder. She was arrested repeatedly. The cycle of arrests and incarceration exacerbated her underlying conditions. According to the report *Who Pays?*, approximately half of all Black transgender people have been incarcerated at some point. Transgender and gender nonconforming people are disproportionately denied opportunities for parole, resulting in their receiving longer sentences than others and adversely impacting them as they struggle to reenter society and secure employment. It also negatively affects their families, who must provide for them during their periods of incarceration.

Criminalizing the poor creates a wider net of poverty than we might imagine. Something as simple as deciding what day a poor person returns to court can drive them deeper into the system. Sometimes court dates are computer generated or selected by an employee. The simple act of asking, "Does this day work for you, ma'am?" gives the defendant an opportunity to say, "Judge, I have a doctor's appointment on that day." Or "Judge, my check and arrives at the first of the month. I won't have any money to get here otherwise. Can I come back one week later?" If we stick to a rigid system of assigning dates without consideration for how people may be affected, we make it harder for them to comply. The effects of these events have a lasting impact.

***

Some cases clearly show the confluence of poverty, trauma, and the criminal justice system. One day, during a conference in my chambers, the public defender entered, scratching his head, and said, "Judge, the defendant said to tell you that you know the man who raped her from the age of twelve to sixteen."

Shocked, I retorted, "What kind of foolishness is she talking about?"

When the public defender mentioned the man's name, I fell back in my chair. My breath left me as if I had been struck in the chest. Who didn't know about the longtime Newark city employee who'd been charged with sexually molesting his niece? He had pled guilty in superior court to a reduced charge. Now, about fifteen years later, the victim, Michelle Smalls, was in my court.

Dear God, why would you send her into my court? What could I possibly do for her? I wondered quietly.

The child of a drug addict, Ms. Smalls had an uncle who stepped in to allegedly help raise her. But, like most sexual predators, he was merely grooming her, gaining her trust. Upon being convicted of a lesser offense, he received probation and wasn't subject to Megan's Law, which mandates registration as a sex offender. While Ms. Smalls struggled to find and maintain work to support her young child, her assailant maintained his lifestyle and used financial leverage to control her. He employed her at a job where he served as a supervisor, and then he fired her.

During one of her court dates, she mentioned that she was delivering food from a local Chinese restaurant, much to my chagrin. I warned her that the job was too dangerous as there had been a rash of attacks and robberies against delivery drivers. (This was when delivery drivers still conducted cash transactions with customers in person, so they carried large amounts of money.) Within a month, the public defender handed me photos of Ms. Smalls with bruises on her face and a busted lip. She'd been robbed and beaten while delivering food.

Despite these challenges, she successfully completed her court-mandated program and occasionally returned to court with her son to visit. After I hadn't seen her for a while, she appeared before me one day with traffic tickets. I noticed that she had become heavy, and her youthful spark was gone. A couple of weeks later the public defender shared with me that Ms. Smalls had died.

Soon after, I stood over Ms. Smalls's body as it lay peacefully in the casket. I thought, *The mortician didn't even get her complexion right*. He had given her honey-brown skin the color of wheat bread. And he had put her in a silly wig. She would have wanted to be buried in her signature, shoulder-length box braids. That's how I focused my attention to keep from crying at the funeral.

I make it a rule not to attend the funerals of defendants, yet Ms. Smalls was different. I felt overwhelmed by guilt because we—the entire system—had failed her from the time she was a young girl until her last breath. She took up the proverbial popping-prescription-pills habit. It's an expensive addiction, at $25 a pill. The day came when she couldn't scrape up the money for a pill and she turned to heroin, the cheaper, more accessible alternative at $5 a bag. It was as if her heart were a time bomb whose detonation was triggered by the drug. The first time she used heroin, she went into cardiac arrest. She was found face down on her lawn. In an attempt to get help, she had somehow made her way back home. I wonder if people passing by saw her lying on the ground. Did they write her off as another hapless addict unworthy of concern? In poor neighborhoods, it's not unusual to see high or drunk people lying around. People are accustomed to ignoring them.

Dead at around thirty years old. Her story was tragic but unfortunately not uncommon. A study of adverse childhood experiences (ACEs) found a strong correlation between childhood exposure to abuse or household dysfunction and adult "health risk behavior" and disease. The study questionnaire asked the nearly ten thousand participants about past childhood exposure to factors including substance abuse by parents or caregivers, mental illness of parents or caregivers, violent treatment of mother or stepmother, and criminal behavior in the household. Over half the respondents (52 percent) had been exposed to at least one ACE, most commonly to substance abuse. Individuals who were exposed to any single category of ACE were also exposed to another category. Adults who had experienced multiple categories of ACEs had increased risk for alcoholism, drug abuse, and suicidal tendencies. The study also concluded that a significant relationship existed between exposure to trauma as a child and various risk factors for leading causes of death in adults, including heart disease and cancer. Its findings are of critical importance because they show that abuse, neglect, and other damaging childhood experiences contribute to adults developing health and lifestyle risk factors, illness, and mortality.[8]

Self-destructive behaviors, like alcohol and drug abuse, are coping mechanisms people use to deal with past childhood trauma. Unfortunately, these inclinations can lead to early death. As a child, Ms. Smalls had been exposed to substance abuse through her mother and had endured sexual abuse by her uncle. Those adverse experiences increased her own risk for abusing drugs. As a result, it doesn't seem implausible to assert that they had a direct connection to shortening her life. Being aware of this information gives us a better understanding of the people who come through our courts. In many cases, they need support.

***

Poverty can also cause intergenerational incarceration. I saw this clearly in the case of one young drug dealer who appeared before me. I heard Chris Cowing's case in the morning. When I finished, he didn't leave the courtroom. Instead, he returned to his seat and sat there all morning. In the afternoon, when the prisoners were brought into the courtroom to have their cases resolved, he stood up and told me that he was there on behalf of his dad. It crushed my heart. When I looked at the father's criminal record, there were already similarities to the son's shorter one. Both began the same way, with arrests and charges for drug distribution. The father's record veered into other offenses after his prison stint, to include drug possession, criminal trespass, and theft, charges often signaling drug use. The drug dealer had become his own best client.

This scenario replays itself repeatedly with other father-son defendants. What must it mean for a young man to see his father emerge from the holding room shackled to another human being? The father, drug sick, is filthy from running the streets, looking to score drugs. The son often doesn't have enough money to post bail. The worst part is that the son may be watching his own future play out before his eyes.

Given the opportunity, people often live better than we expect them to. So we have to change how we impose our expectations on them. If poverty drives someone to become a nuisance, that alone can't justify criminalizing their behavior. True, we don't want homeless people sleeping in the public park. But levying fines, court costs, and inevitably jail for failing to pay those fines is an illogical response.

When considering monetary penalties that will be uncollectible and will worsen the person's state, prosecutors must make reasonable offers and judges must consider other options. First, the judge should consider imposing community service in lieu of a monetary penalty or converting existing monetary penalties to community service. More specifically, the judge should recommend the individual to a community service site that is easily accessible and can provide them with services. In

Newark, we were able to increase defendants' access to social services through community service sentencing. We assisted nonprofits to become approved community service sites.

The reforms I'm suggesting here don't require major financial investments. They do, however, require practitioners to heighten their understanding and awareness. When the traditional procedures seem inadequate, common sense must prevail. We need to resist the pressure to rush, and instead take time to ensure that a person's dignity remains intact and they are given a path out of the cycles of incarceration and even deeper poverty.

Without a change in our thinking and approach, people will continue to be trapped by poverty and the criminal justice system. How we currently operate ignores how poverty drives individuals' contacts with that system. It ignores how laws are created to target the poor, or how application of those laws condemns them. As a result, the judge and the defendant coexist in a shared hallucination, with the judge imposing an impossible obligation to pay and the defendant unrealistically agreeing to pay. Overreliance on financial penalties undermines the court's relationship with the community while also breaking the spirit of its citizens.

The next chapter offers a strategy for addressing the problem of poverty trapping people in the criminal justice system. It discusses the impact Newark Community Solutions, Newark's community court project, has made on both the city and its residents.

Chapter 5

REFORMS THAT TRANSFORM

"**Y**our eyes look sad, Judge," Jamal Bigelow said as he twisted his fingers around strands of his voluminous black hair, which had been recently streaked with a blond patch.

I was surprised; I was usually better at keeping my composure in court. "I am sad," I said, touched by his concern. "You are not doing well, and I don't know what to do to help you." I looked at him and rested my chin on my hand.

I had just witnessed the twenty-two-year-old stomp his feet three times and raise his arms to his sides, like a bird about to take flight. He made this motion while yelling, "Michael Mitchell says to stomp your feet when the spirits talk to you." The voices tormented him today. When the court intern completed Mr. Bigelow's public defender application, he emitted outbursts of laughter, responding to some invisible inner narrator.

Imagine what it would be like to be unable to access the parts of your mind that give you self-control, or even just a sense of peace. Mr. Bigelow battled the voices while he was talking to me. I'd ask him a question, and he'd get this blank look on his face and begin to chuckle.

Finally, attempting to bring his attention back, I said sternly, "Tell the voices I said I'm speaking now." Again, he stared off into the room and then lowered his gaze.

I asked, "What are they saying?"

"They said let them help you."

"Okay. Listen to that. But don't listen if they tell you to hurt yourself or anybody else."

Mr. Bigelow's first contact with my court came when his mother filed a domestic violence simple-assault case against him. When she appeared in court, I learned that she also suffered from mental illness; she was accompanied by her counselor. She started screaming so loudly in the middle of the court session that I had to send her into the hallway.

Two years later, and deeper into the abyss of his mental illness, Mr. Bigelow stood before me on a drug possession charge. Like his other family members who suffered from mental illness and lived with his grandma and used illicit drugs, he had begun to use spice, a synthetic marijuana, to quiet the voices. I remember him telling me that his grandma's kitchen table was covered with crack.

The lack of proper health care prevented the members of Mr. Bigelow's family from fully understanding their mental health conditions. Instead of receiving appropriate care, they had embraced a legacy of misinformation for generations. It's as though they were sharing a homeopathic remedy for mental illness, except the cure pushed them into the criminal justice system and could ultimately lead to their deaths.

Mr. Bigelow kept saying, "I'm so happy to be here seeing you, Judge. I love you, Judge." I believed him.

Fortunately for Mr. Bigelow, I sent him to the Newark Community Solutions program. I gave him eight court-ordered days for evaluation, and after meeting with the case compliance specialist, he was assigned a social worker. His social worker was able to get him admitted into an excellent day program run by the Rutgers Behavioral Health Program at Rutgers University Hospital. He attended daily and received counseling and medication. They even taught him to play an instrument. I monitored his progress for a couple of months to ensure that he attended and remained engaged. His social worker received updates and kept in contact with him. He returned to court a couple of times, and the program provided a progress report. Once we felt he was stabilized, the prosecutor dismissed his case.

"I'm very proud of you, Mr. Bigelow," I told him that day.

"I'm proud of myself, Judge," he responded. He never returned to court with a new case.

Poverty often appears together with mental health disorders, and in low-level cases like Mr. Bigelow's, people respond better to support and treatment than they do to jail or prison time. Newark Community Solutions gives the justice system the ability to respond effectively to a number of community issues, including the types of mental health crises that drive people to the courthouse.

In a traditional court, the judge engages a defendant who has mental health issues without being able to address those issues. The condition is usually the root cause of the offense that brings them to court. In many instances, judges will request a mental health evaluation to document whether there is a history of mental illness. Unfortunately, the report arrives without any specific instruction about how to handle the defendant or where to send them to receive assistance. Alternative sentencing options, administered through community courts, provide the best outcomes for those suffering from mental illness and the best resolutions for courts.

***

In 2006, after an embattled mayoral election for the city's heart, Newark, New Jersey, underwent a changing of the guard. The former mayor had declined to run again, and it was the first time in twenty-five years the city would have new leadership. I knocked on doors to help campaign for the progressive ticket of candidates that swept into office. Lifetime Newarkers had new energy, a new plan, and had to welcome new faces.

At the beginning of his term, then Mayor, now Senator, Cory Booker sent a newspaper clipping to then Newark Municipal Court's Chief Judge, now Federal District Judge, Julien Neals. The article detailed the benefits of the community court program that operated in New York City. Mayor Booker, a devoted longtime crusader for criminal justice reform, had set the wheels in motion to change how justice would be delivered in Newark. My boss, Council President Mildred Crump, brought a blue spiral notebook to my office and placed it on one of the piles on my desk.

She said, "Cory's interested in doing this. Tell me what you think." Little did I know that her request was a prelude to a decision that would change the course of my life.

After visiting the Red Hook Community Justice Center in Brooklyn, I was enthusiastic about the possibility of bringing something similar to our city. I witnessed how Judge Alex Calabrese spoke to defendants so respectfully. I was amazed at how comfortable they were talking to him. He subsequently became one of my mentors. Building a community court in Newark was going to be wonderful for the entire community.

After four hard and long years, the superior court and the administrative office of the court decided to allow Newark to create a community court program. I pursued the role of municipal court judge. That meant I had to lobby people around the mayor for their support to obtain a nomination. One day, while sitting in Mayor Booker's office for a meeting, I realized I had only one option—to ask the mayor directly for what I wanted. I have to admit, I was one of those people who hated the word "no" so profoundly that I resisted making requests just to avoid hearing it. The romance novelist Nora Roberts has said, "If you don't ask, the answer is always no." I took a deep breath and asked. And because the mayor's aim was to infuse the city with new ideas and a new approach, he agreed. Ultimately, my appointment would lead to my serving as the state's and the city's first community court judge and to my being the first judge of Dominican descent.

Before the city established the community court, an organization called the Center for Court Innovation (CCI) held meetings across Newark to receive input from residents about what they wanted justice to look like at the municipal court. Surprisingly, residents were not interested in having the municipal court impose more punishment. Instead, they wanted the court to provide more *assistance* to the residents who came through its doors. They wanted the young men hanging out on the corners in their neighborhoods to have opportunities to get jobs and continue their education. They wanted the drug addicts who were nodding out in their neighborhoods to get treatment so they could improve their lives. What I realized is that these individuals were their neighbors. The residents wanted to reintegrate these people into their community, not cast them further out into the margins.

The problem-solving court model takes a preventive posture: it attempts to prevent crime by resolving the underlying issues that cause the unlawful behavior. This contrasts with the traditional model, which focuses solely on ruling on narrow legal issues or on punishment after the fact.[1]

One of the country's first community courts, the Midtown Community Court, established in Midtown Manhattan in 1993, worked to tackle small issues. Local business owners, city officials, and law enforcement agents who were fed up with low-level quality-of-life crimes—graffiti, turnstile jumping, prostitution, public intoxication—decided to join forces to come up with a solution. My mom would walk me and my younger brother down Manhattan's 42nd Street toward the Port Authority Bus Terminal while yelling, "Look straight ahead," and often covering our eyes, so I had witnessed the den of inequities in that part of the city. The coming together of community, business, and government stakeholders set the stage for what we would see in cities and towns across the country that were advancing toward community justice. The CCI was born of this collaboration. A beacon of light and champion for improving the delivery of justice, the CCI has sounded the alarm for reform for decades and has worked with jurisdictions and communities to provide the solutions—from the reduction of mass incarceration, to improving justice, to reducing violence—all the while providing data and honoring the needs and desires of the community. Their work on the Midtown Community Court and the Red Hook Community

Justice Center provided the foundational model for what we would do in Newark.

Jethro Antoine was appointed as the founding director of Newark Community Solutions. He is now the national director of technical support. A longtime advocate of the project, he presented the idea to the Newark City Council in coordination with Adam Mansky of the CCI and representatives of the New Jersey Institute for Social Justice. His first hire, Kelly Mulligan-Brown as court resource coordinator, now program director and director of New Jersey programs, started one week after I was assigned to criminal courtroom 222, the arraignment court and the future home of the community court. Reflecting on the creation of the program, Mr. Antoine said, "Newark Community Solutions was the product of collaboration among the Center for Court Innovation, the leadership of the city of Newark, a dedicated group of community leaders, and neighborhood activists. The project continues to prosper because those actors remain at the table."

Ms. Mulligan-Brown said, "When I started with Newark Community Solutions, when we were just a program on paper, I wanted to help create a system in Newark that didn't let people slip through the cracks but rather lifted them up to get the help they needed. Now, over ten years later, I am more convinced than ever that community justice programs are a key component of effective and human-centered criminal justice reform in America."

Newark Community Solutions—made up of a team of social workers, caseworkers, a coordinator, and other criminal justice specialists—partners with the courts to provide judges with alternative sentencing options that expand possibilities for dealing with low-level, nonviolent offenders. It does this by offering a range of community service, counseling, and treatment options. The clinic created by the program uses a client-centered and trauma-informed approach to providing services. As always, the secret sauce is the enthusiastic, highly skilled, service-oriented professionals. When hiring them, Director Antoine worked to ensure that these visionaries, with their can-do attitudes, served the entire community. They tried and tried again with the participants. They found a way when there previously had been no way.

Tonya Tucker, a veteran frontline social worker, had worked with local nonprofits for twelve years before joining Newark Community Solutions. Born and raised in Newark, her insight was invaluable; she often took on the more demanding cases. When asked about the difference between Newark Community Solutions and other places where she had worked, she said, "Newark Community Solutions was able to bring options to a community that didn't know they had options. Newark Community Solutions gave the community a sounding board, gave them social workers, officers, and most importantly a judge that would come off the bench and embrace them with opportunities. It changed the courtroom environment, the courthouse, in a way that made people in the community want to know what this community court was all about."

Managing the day-to-day operations was our skillful court resource coordinator, Janet Idrogo. Petite and soft-spoken, she was the face of the program and also its hammer. She started with Newark Community Solutions as a college intern and fell in love with the work. She said:

I had the privilege of bearing witness to people changing their lives on a daily basis, literally. I saw the defendant's first interaction with Judge, and often they were defiant and disrespectful. (Symptoms of a broken system.) And in a future court date, that same person would lay out their soul in the form of an essay and ultimately often end with gratitude for the experience. We underestimate what having a voice really means in today's world. I went into this work to ensure that people going through the system were heard in a place where they were otherwise often muted and dismissed. With the leadership of Judge Pratt and countless partners in the courthouse, that space became alive. Since then, many courts have adopted similar practices, both national and international, truly pioneering what is possible in this field. What this meant for me was giving me the opportunity to be a partner in change in a world that seemed untouchable.

The diversity of the staff's experiences was an asset. Our first clinical director, Sienna Hunter-Cuyjet, was a community outreach dynamo. She made alliances using her knowledge and understanding as a First Nations woman who grew up on a reservation in New York State.

Our next clinical director, Colleen Smith, who is now the program's deputy director, brought another distinctive perspective. She said:

Before Newark Community Solutions, I worked with people who were incarcerated [at Essex County Jail]. They were either serving a sentence or detained pending trial. In sessions, we would speak at length about what someone would do "when I get out," but it was all hypothetical. When I started at Newark Community Solutions—where my clients remained in the community as I provided services—we could work toward goals together, and I could provide support when things did not go as planned. I could advocate. It's hard to advocate when you're behind bars—even when you're the social worker.

Raul Hernandez, the community site supervisor, spent hours speaking potential into the participants' lives as they complained, lamented, reflected, or mulled over their situations. He said, "We diligently searched for community service sites that were meaningful, places with people who cared. We wanted our participants to leave with not only a change in perspective but a change of heart as well."

Another Newark native and longtime community activist, Karimah Williams, joined the staff as an alternative sanctions specialist. "Being an activist for my community," she said, "I was able to be married to my community and the law, and we were able to save some broken souls, through love, compassion, empathy, and being a good listener."

Among the folks who know the value of Newark Community Solutions best are the defendants who have completed their programs. Some improved so dramatically, and believed in the program so fully, that they joined the program's staff, like Trevor Powell. "The arrest that led me to the program saved my life," he said recently. He had been dealing pot for the quick money and the allure of the risky lifestyle, but his decisions led him down a rabbit hole that he couldn't get out of. He dropped out of his second year of college after his grades began to slip and found himself with a large amount of

student debt. He worked as a baggage handler, security officer, and sales associate while addressing the debt. Soon he was
arrested on possession of a marijuana cigarette.

His youthful face, fresh haircut with compact waves, and
stiffly pressed business suit made him stand out in court. After
admitting him to the program, I immediately assigned him an
essay. He asked for help getting back into school. Ms. Smith, his
social worker, assisted him with enrollment in Essex County
College.

The courtroom was captivated when Mr. Powell read his
riveting and deeply personal response to my essay assignment,
"How Good and Bad Decisions Have Affected My Life." He
described how his poor choices had hurt so many of the people
he loved.

> Somehow, I was able to keep my cell phone while I was in
> the holding cell. My phone rang, and it was my girlfriend's
> 3-year-old daughter calling from her mother's phone. Her
> mom would put her on the line to help her call me whenever
> she wanted me to bring her food or even a toy. That day, she
> just asked for a snack. I loved her like she was my own child.
> Here's this child who looks up to me, and I can't even get her
> what she needs because I'm sitting here locked up. I didn't
> answer. I just teared up. Everything changed from that point
> on. I knew what got me here.

I had to wait for the applause to die down before I could
comment. It was Mr. Powell's last day, and he had successfully
completed the program. I instructed Ms. Idrogo, the court resource coordinator, to give him a business card so he could
interview to serve as an intern. As a court intern, he worked

three days a week while holding down his security job. "It felt really great being a part of something good. And after a few weeks of working there, I knew I wanted to make it a career," he said.

Mr. Powell remembers having to cut off some previous relationships to change his path. He was surprised when people who knew him from before saw that he was working at the courthouse and said, "This is what you should have been doing all the time." The program administrators were so impressed with his work that they asked him to interview for the community service site supervisor job. He was offered the position after beating out other candidates in a series of interviews. He continues to work there, run a business, and serve his community.

***

The court's goal in partnering with Newark Community Solutions is twofold: to significantly reduce the use of jail while simultaneously reducing the commission of offenses. Unlike a traditional court, community courts have a resource coordinator stationed in the courtroom. This staff member identifies defendants who are candidates for the program based on a review of criminal records, cursory interviews, and current open charges. They impart information from the clinic to the court and vice versa. As the face and voice of the clinic, the resource coordinator reads aloud the clinic's suggestions and provides participants' compliance updates during their court appearances.

Instead of using money as the basis for punishment, Newark Community Solutions leans into community service to allow defendants to earn credit for the money they owe. Although imposing community service isn't novel in criminal justice sentencing, our approach to community service is vastly different. With the idea of restoring the community at the forefront, the court can mandate defendants to highly visible, and beneficial, community service projects in residential neighborhoods and business districts. Residents can see the work and attribute it to the court program. Defendants wear mesh vests to identify themselves as a part of the Newark Community Solutions community service crew. The program shows that the justice system acknowledges the defendant's harm to the neighborhood and is taking action to address the harm caused by the wrongdoing.

Relying heavily on community service permits the court to provide punishment with assistance. Assistance comes through social service mandates, which are tailored to fit each defendant's underlying needs, and can include job referrals, literacy programs, GED programs, mental health evaluations, and housing assistance. From a more stable position, defendants can start to live a better life. There are also individual and group counseling sessions, drug treatment, treatment readiness classes, and monitored placement in community-based treatment programs. Led by facilitators, counseling groups consist of talk therapy sessions that focus on a specific topic. There are several different groups, including a women's group, a group for sexual health education, and a young men's group. Professor Tyrell Connor, PhD, of City University of New York, who spent time observing my practices in the courtroom, ran the young men's group, named the Fire Next Time (after James Baldwin's book). Men between ages eighteen and twenty-five, assigned to the group as a part of their mandates, often came from rival gangs or sects. Their sessions were so productive that the participants would spill onto the courthouse steps after exceeding the session's time in the meeting room. The group gave them a safe and confidential space where they could express themselves.

Newark Community Solutions offers its resources to the whole community, not just to those who've committed offenses. The program accepts walk-ins even if they do not have active court cases. This meant we could treat an entire family. A participant in the program who was charged with selling drugs might bring his father who had a drug dependency issue to see his social worker. Now Dad could get connected to detox and substance abuse treatment while his son got his life on track. This open-door policy also supported reentry efforts: formerly incarcerated individuals could walk out of jail or prison, go directly to the courthouse, and enter the clinic. Once there, they could speak to a social worker or caseworker and immediately get help with obtaining identification, housing, governmental monetary assistance, and referrals and appointments to other programs.

Newark Community Solutions' expanded sentencing options have also reduced the court's dependence on ill-imposed fines and fees and the overuse of jail for minor offenses. For example, a shoplifter with an underlying mental health issue can receive short-term individual counseling on-site, accompanied by referral to and placement in a community-based program. Participants' needs are identified after a review of their criminal record, a conversation with their attorney, an exchange with the judge, a psychosomatic evaluation, and a meeting with their caseworkers and social workers. The social workers and caseworkers are housed at the courthouse, and participants in the program are sent directly to meet with them upon leaving the courtroom. Defendants not only are offered ways to heal their trauma, mental issues, or drug dependency; they are put on a path toward contributing to their families and to society.

Our partnership with the Newark Downtown Business District was one of many we had that focused on employment. Comprising corporations, businesses, and community leaders who want to encourage people to shop and socialize in downtown Newark, the organization is responsible for beautifying the area. It had previously outsourced the hiring of its street-cleaning team. The subcontractor observed our community service workers, many of whom the company invited to apply for permanent and seasonal positions. With additional staff, the organization could clean and maintain larger areas. The partnership both offered the employer a great opportunity to show support for our program and connected former offenders to employment, helping them overcome the stigma of incarceration and involvement with the justice system. Other benefits included the fact that beautification of the business district would translate to increased revenues for businesses and taxes for the city.

One program participant who was hired as a permanent employee was Michelle Broad, a military veteran whose PTSD had led her to become addicted to heroin. I would see her in her bright yellow shirt, pushing her wheeled can, helping to maintain the same streets where she once had bought drugs and spread litter. (Interestingly, many of the defendants who performed community service downtown were helping to clean up a part of the city where they had committed their offenses.) I would chat with her about the job and about her sobriety as I walked through the area in the afternoon. Ms. Broad had been recognized for her strengths as a member of the military, including her extreme work ethic. She brought her talents as a soldier to her new job.

Occasionally, a defendant who completed the program through a community partnership would tell us that they still experienced discrimination in the job market. Social stigma and hiring discrimination are among the worst of the collateral consequences of having a criminal record, and those penalties can remain with a person long after they've worked to get on a better path. People with criminal convictions also face legal restrictions that prevent them from having access to housing, education, and welfare, from obtaining professional licenses, and from other prospects.

In addition to assisting with job opportunities and other services, Newark Community Solutions has a goal to improve public safety. The program has partnered with local law enforcement agencies to help them provide solutions to the social problems they encounter. As a result, to list just two examples, the New Jersey Transit Police hired a social worker to serve individuals who live at Penn Station, and the Newark Police Department received a grant to create a program for diverting certain opioid-related offenses.

Another feature that distinguishes community court from traditional court is the weekly meeting that takes place between court players, program employees, and the judge to discuss participants who are not doing well in the program or who may need immediate attention. The team includes the prosecutor, the public defender, and the probation officer. The Newark Community Solutions staff who attend are the director, the clinical director, a social worker, the resource coordinator, and occasionally the community service site supervisor. At a typical meeting, the social worker may report that, for instance, an individual has an immediate medical need that should be addressed before their next court date. The judge may waive their next court appearance so they can get into treatment or undergo a procedure. The compliance specialist may report that an individual had a problem at the community service site with another participant or the host. The public defender may argue on their behalf while the prosecutor may argue that the person should be removed from the program. The team can also discuss ways to turn someone around and ensure compliance.

The problem-solving approach to justice cultivated by community courts like Newark Community Solutions fosters a relationship between the court and the community by connecting defendants to services. The program's relationships with the state-level public defender's office and prosecutor's office allow the municipal court to extend its reach and better manage defendants with multiple charges.

The Center for Court Innovation, the parent organization, assigned a researcher to the project whose role is to work with Newark Community Solutions to design research projects and produce reports. This collection of data is useful for evaluating the effectiveness of the program and the courthouse's relationship to the people it serves.

***

Among our many initiatives, Newark Community Solutions joined forces with local nonprofits and Newark residents who were tackling the issue of food insecurity. This was helpful in the case of James Potts, a serial panhandler who operated on the Martin Luther King, Jr. exit ramp of Route 280. The victim of a robbery that turned into a vicious beating, Mr. Potts suffered from a traumatic brain injury that left him functioning at the mental level of an adolescent. In his mid-fifties with a slight frame, graying hair, and slurred speech, he was unable to perform routine functions such as reading and remembering. With lowered gaze and slurred speech, he told me that his son had entered foster care following the assault. After three years of rehabilitation and fighting the system, he regained custody of his son.

Months later, Mr. Potts returned to court on multiple panhandling cases. My patience had waned. I demanded to know why he continued to pick up these cases. I was sure he received government assistance monthly, and he didn't pick up drug charges, so he was not panhandling to buy drugs.

His response shook me to my core. He said, "Judge, my son is a big boy, and he eats through the food stamps we get quick." Those of you with growing teenagers can relate. We immediately sent Mr. Potts to a neighborhood food pantry to perform community service. There, he would receive a bag of groceries after a day of service and could return on other days to supplement the food he had at home.

Government assistance is not a large amount of money. And with his injuries, Mr. Potts couldn't conceptualize other options for increasing his income to supplement the food he could purchase. I had to step out of my personal frustration with the person and listen. Even though I and the officers issuing the panhandling tickets had lost our patience with Mr. Potts, we needed to ask why he continued to panhandle. Additionally, community service participants who work at a soup kitchen or community food bank gain access to other services.

Newark Community Solutions partnered with residents participating in the city's Adopt-a-Lot program, which allowed local residents to become responsible for the upkeep of an abandoned lot on their block. In most instances, residents turned the lots into community gardens that offered free fruit and vegetables to the neighbors. In a food desert like parts of Newark, this was remarkable. Program participants cleared the lots of garbage, cultivated the soil, and planted seeds. They learned about horticulture.

After witnessing the success of these community gardens, I am astounded to see urban gardens come under fire. Critics attacked the description in Michelle Obama's book of the White House vegetable garden, calling it elitist. This criticism was unfounded. It reminded me of a conversation with a colleague who asked, "What do you say to critics who say you are imposing upper-middle-class values on poor people?"

I raised my eyebrow as a smile spread across my face. "Guess what? Poor people have values too. And if you ask poor people, they will probably tell you they have more values than people with money. Because they share the little that they have to ensure someone eats or has what they need. That is a true sacrifice, a selfless act. Their neighbors eat and survive because of their generosity and sense of responsibility to one another."

Ascribing a class designation to people's value system is, at best, illogical. Gardens help people come together and meet communal goals by pooling their physical resources. The resulting produce is offered to the entire community at no cost. The community service workers get to repay the debt they owe, and the community gains a valuable resource. Critics are somehow suggesting that poor people don't understand or value the benefits of fresh produce and good nutrition. They ignore the fact that poor and working-class people often live in food deserts without access to supermarkets and fresh fruit and vegetables. The city of Newark had been without a major grocery store for twenty-three years until 1990, when a new Pathmark opened there. The previous supermarket had been destroyed in the 1967 rebellions. Now the city has a ShopRite, a Whole Foods, and a Bravo supermarket, to name a few. Even so, critics often fail to acknowledge that the poor and working class are usually priced out of buying fresh produce.

Newark Community Solutions helps resolve local problems that find their way into the justice system. Its status as a nonprofit also allows it to collaborate and bring ideas and innovations to all criminal justice professionals and community stakeholders.

***

When I called Shani Star's name, I was astonished by her disrespectful attitude, the way she laughed and joked with people in the courtroom as she sashayed her way down the aisle. She went out of her way to strut, even while bearing a surgical boot on her left foot. She wore black leggings and a colorful sweatshirt, and when she finally made it to counsel's table, I noticed the tattoo on her left temple, accompanied by another below it. I knew she was going to be a challenge.

Ms. Star was charged with being a disorderly person. She looked back over her right shoulder toward the audience when she said her name for the record, like a contestant on a televised game show, giving the people what they want. She performed to attract the attention of the men in the courtroom. If I'd seen this behavior once, I'd seen it a thousand times. I, however, require order, as she would quickly learn.

I asked about the injury to her foot.

She smiled proudly and boasted, "Oh yeah, Judge, I got shot in my foot."

Ms. Star didn't act as if she thought she was a victim. In fact, she reminded me of the young men who regarded their bullet wounds, or their nights in jail, as badges of honor. They actually called it getting their "stripes," as though they had served in the military.

When I asked for further details, she explained, "Judge, I was just standing outside, and somebody came by and started shooting up the place. I just got hit."

For some reason I did not believe her. They must have targeted her and missed.

I asked, "You do realize someone was trying to murder you? They just had bad aim."

I admitted her to the program and gave her a new court date. I also sent her off with an admonishment: "Make it your business to stay inside since people are shooting at you. I don't want them to accidentally shoot and hurt anyone else. You should also stay off the foot so that it heals."

When Ms. Star returned for her next appointment, Ms. Idrogo, the court resource coordinator, reported that she had failed to attend any of her court-ordered mandates.

Ms. Star said, "Oh, I couldn't make it because my foot was hurting. I had on these cute shoes and they hurt my feet, ha ha ha." She swung her body back and forth to get a reaction from the audience.

Lord, give me strength. Someone forgot to tell Ms. Star that I was the only cute person in the courtroom, so if she was vying for the job it was already taken.

After watching her theatrics and hearing her excuses, I realized that assisting her would be even more difficult than I originally had thought. I gave her additional mandated counseling days. Hopefully that would give the team ample time to get to the source of her issue. But on her next reporting day she failed to show, and I issued a bench warrant for her arrest.

Soon after, Ms. Star showed up at the appointment window to have her matter rescheduled before another judge. She didn't realize I had written a note on her file: "Only schedule before Judge Pratt." The court administrator marched her directly into my courtroom. It's amazing how quickly people can muster up contriteness and humility when they have an open bench warrant and want to avoid being arrested on the spot.

Ms. Star was still in shock when she appeared before me that day, and none of her usual sass was on display. After I gave her a stern reprimand and reminded her once again that she was putting innocent bystanders' lives at risk, including her daughter's, the message finally seemed to hit home. The threat of arrest may have helped deliver the reality check. The truth was that her recklessness was endangering not only herself but those she loved.

She most likely knew who shot her. However, she was living by the "no-snitch" code of the streets, which shielded her assailant as much as it protected her. Rumors circulate wildly about the harm that comes to people who share incriminating information with the authorities. But after signing so many warrants for probable cause and reading police reports with statements implicating co-conspirators, I knew that the no-snitch rule was mostly a façade used by some to subjugate others. Yes, many people lived by it, but I found that people were often quick to save themselves in exchange for a reduced sentence.

Ms. Star's subsequent court appearances were very different from her initial ones. It seemed like her respectful and sweet representative showed up at her community service and her individual and group counseling sessions. In the end, beneath the veneer of a tough, flippant woman lay an introspective and interesting person. She was in total compliance and completely engaged with her social worker. She said she enjoyed the counseling groups because she was able to speak to others who shared experiences similar to hers.

One day she shocked me by walking into the courtroom wearing a jacket and trousers, with her hair pulled back in a long ponytail and makeup covering her facial tattoo.

"You look fabulous," I told her. Even the court administrator complimented her. She glowed with pride.

She looked up at me. "Judge, can I speak?"

"Of course you can. This is a conversation," I reassured her.

"I noticed that people treat you differently when you dress like this. They treat you with more respect. People look at you with more respect. They don't talk to you about your body."

I must admit, until that day I hadn't really noticed how she dressed. It looked like the urban-chic fashion that came through the court all day. Although Ms. Star had grown accustomed to drawing the attention of men, egging on their catcalls and whistles, it didn't make her feel respected.

When she returned to read her essay, she again blew us away. I had assigned her to write a reaction to stories from *Misguided Justice: The War on Drugs and the Incarceration of Black Women.*[2] I wanted her to think about how her relationships with men had led to bad decision-making. Instead, she decided to share her own experience, retitling her essay "By Any Means Necessary." She wrote about her devotion to her boyfriend, in which she essentially played the role of the "ride-or-die chick"—a woman who has her boyfriend's or husband's back no matter what, even at the cost of injury or danger to herself. I meet them when they end up in my court, alone, facing jail for offenses they didn't commit and confused and frightened by the impending consequences.

Ms. Star reminisced about the lengths she had gone through for her boyfriend. Then she realized that he would protect himself and his illicit business at all costs—by any means necessary—including sacrificing her and her daughter. Her words were raw, honest, and reflective. She received a standing ovation.

As is true in many cases, the end of Ms. Star's involvement with our court was marked by both a sense of accomplishment and an uneasiness. Newark Community Solutions and the court had become her extended circle. I worried that she, like others who experienced these short interventions, might easily succumb to the pressures of her life and quickly revert to prior behavior. She had begun to acclimate to new ideas about how she could live. What happens when you are no longer compelled to return to court? What happens when you no longer have a scheduled appointment to discuss your problems and brainstorm ideas to solve them?

Unbeknownst to me, the court resource coordinator, Ms. Idrogo, had been so impressed by Ms. Star's essay and her progress that she asked her to interview to serve as an intern for Newark Community Solutions. Her social worker helped her prepare a resume. After two successful interviews, she prevailed.

Always on time, she became a weekly fixture in courtroom 222. Her duties included entering data in the program's database. More importantly, she spoke with candidates about the requirements and benefits of participating in the program. To see her interact with the candidates with such professionalism gave me immeasurable pride. She had recently been in their shoes, and now she was telling them to trust the process because it had helped her. Now she sat on the other side of the court-room, not judging them but helping them get the assistance they needed, while she continued working on herself. She felt useful and significant. She purchased a sewing machine and started a small online clothing business.

People can be more than we initially see. And the justice system should allow them to be more than the act that brings them to court. In particular, with low-level offenses, the court's interactions with individuals should return them to the com-munity in a better, more productive state. By preserving a hu-man being's dignity rather than damaging it, we increase their value to themselves and society.

On the flip side, people can also have larger problems than we initially see, as in the case of Robin Mader. A portly white woman who appeared to be in her late sixties, she wore reading glasses and was dressed professionally, with gray curls that were almost feathered around her full, oval face. When her name was called, she heaved herself out of the row and took a few seconds to establish her footing. She limped toward counsel's table.

In a flash, I had a vision of her sitting in the county jail, slumped over, defeated, wearing an ill-fitting orange jumpsuit. The outfit was two sizes too small, the rough material looked uncomfortable, and the buttons strained to hold back her girth.

I opened her file to view her charges. She didn't look like she could be an addict. Her rosy face seemed to belong to an unpoisoned body. I saw that she had three open shoplifting charges for stealing scarves from the Metropolitan Museum of Art store at Newark Liberty International Airport. In New Jersey, three convictions for shoplifting carried a mandatory ninety-day jail sentence, in addition to fines, costs, and mandatory fees. Somehow, someone writing the shoplifting legislation had unscientifically arrived at the conclusion that after three convictions, a jail sentence of three months would set the shoplifter straight.

Ms. Mader's case had been transferred from another courtroom. The judge must've seen exactly what I saw and sent her case to my court with hopes that she would be admitted to the program. As I looked at the grandmother standing before me, I knew that the legislators had never dreamed the shoplifting law would entangle the likes of this woman, who could be their own mother or grandmother, in the criminal justice system.

The prosecutor and the public defender requested that she be admitted to the court program. She stood with her eyes downcast and tense. I imagined that she avoided eye contact because she felt embarrassed. I was embarrassed for her. She agreed to participate in the program. She didn't want to gamble with a trial in which she might lose big. I ordered additional social services, with no community service. First, her limp would make it nearly impossible for her to complete community service, and second, she needed to undergo a deeper dive with the social workers and counseling groups.

I learned that she had a very successful consulting business that trained executives from Fortune 500 companies. Clearly she didn't have to resort to stealing items from a store. Yet when she flew out of Newark Liberty to her consulting jobs, she invariably stopped at the Metropolitan Museum store and stole high-priced scarves, $125 a piece. I never learned what triggered the behavior, but perhaps an earlier trauma had lain dormant and unaddressed for some time.

During her review sessions, she appeared to be enjoying herself. She clapped vigorously when people read their essays or reported landing a job interview. She seemed relieved when she came up for her compliance hearings, and I praised her for putting in the work. An experience that probably kept her up at night had turned into something good. It's possible that the courtroom became something different for her—something besides a place that dispenses punishment. Because she participated in Newark Community Solutions, perhaps court became a place of treatment and healing, not extreme judgment. Yes, I wanted her to stop stealing and causing harm to the merchant. However, I knew that would only happen if we uncovered and addressed the "why." Why did she steal when she could afford to purchase the item? Why was she triggered by that particular store?

I learned from the social worker that Ms. Mader had been diagnosed with kleptomania. Something in her personal life had triggered the disorder. The Mayo Clinic defines kleptomania as "the recurrent inability to resist urges to steal items that you generally don't really need and that usually have little value."[3] It's categorized as an impulse-control disorder: individuals who have the condition find it impossible to fight the temptation or urge to engage in certain undesired actions. Many people with kleptomania live with an enormous amount of shame. Unfortunately, most people who suffer from the disorder never get diagnosed, despite their numerous encounters with the law and the courts.

Kleptomania is a significant mental health disorder treatable with talk therapy or medication, but it has no cure. It is also quite rare and primarily diagnosed in women. Ms. Mader was an unusual defendant in my criminal courtroom—she was white, privileged, and had resources. She owned a successful business and had clients who valued her and acknowledged her worth. She also lived with the "benefit of the doubt" based on her position in the world. I wondered how many times she had been caught stealing, was allowed to pay for or return the item, and permitted to leave the store without being charged.

The behavior that Ms. Mader engaged in seemed to satisfy an irresistible urge to steal for the sake of stealing. For her, the items she took were unnecessary. However, when one steals because of poverty, the stolen item is usually necessary to meet an immediate need. As a society, we frown upon and judge the person who steals because of poverty more harshly because there is a tendency to blame people for their indigence. If a kleptomaniac's condition creates an irresistible urge to steal, then why can't we believe that a poor person's hunger also creates an irresistible urge to steal a candy bar from the store in Penn Station?

While she stood out from the impoverished thieves who came to my courtroom, Ms. Mader certainly did not receive special treatment. She was required to participate in group and individual counseling sessions like everyone else ordered to the program. The thought of what ninety days in the county jail would have done to her physically and psychologically is unfathomable. Instead of being subjected to confinement, she was given the professional attention and the talk therapy that she needed to manage her compulsions and prevent future offenses. After she completed the program I never saw her again.

Ms. Mader was clearly not similarly situated economically, socially, or racially to her fellow members of the counseling group or even her fellow spectators in the courtroom. What they all had in common, however, was that they suffered from emotional distress that led them into the hands of the criminal justice system. When they most needed it, they received assistance, not harsh punishment, for their conditions.

If the court is viewed as a community resource, and not just a place to be feared, its impact can ripple out into the community in unexpected ways. This hit me one day as I was driving on my usual commute and had stopped at a red light before attempting to make a left turn. I was in a bit of a rush, but I had to cool my heels as I waited for the light to change. A formidable black SUV with opaque, tinted windows pulled up alongside me. I gave the driver's side a measured glance. I noticed the window slowly begin to slide down.

Oh, damn, this never goes well in the movies, I thought and averted my gaze.

As I flipped through my mental Rolodex of possibly provoking deeds from the last week, a voice boomed from the open window, "Hey, Judge Pratt! I've been looking for you. I got an idea for a program to help young men stay out of jail."

I looked closer at the silhouette and recognized the bald head and birthmark. It was Michael Johnson, an OG (old-school gangster) leader in the Bloods.

I opened my car window and jokingly replied, "Lazarus has risen!" I pretended to clutch my pearls.

Wasn't he supposed to be sitting in a federal prison? I thought. *This dude just got out and one of the first places he goes is to the municipal courthouse?* Then I remembered how he had worked with Newark Community Solutions to help squash a beef, a brewing altercation between a court participant and another gang member. A few days after our exchange at the intersection, he

appeared at the courthouse. He sat in the back of the courtroom because he knew he'd get an audience with the judge. He
wanted to do something positive, and if she couldn't help him
get started, at least she would send him to someone who could.
He talked to the Newark Community Solutions representative
about developing a mentorship program. Boy, am I happy I
treat people with dignity and respect.

As Mr. Johnson's story shows, the court and Newark Community Solutions, together, created a space for redemption.
And the courthouse was the place to facilitate it through innovation and partnership. A new level of trust had developed,
and it spread throughout the community. Not only could the
program help someone, but it could help that person help and
heal others.

***

In addition to partnering with social services, civic organizations, and local businesses, Newark Community Services also
partners with houses of worship that have other nonprofit arms
engaged in providing services to the community. Faith-based
institutions have been at the forefront of every social change
movement since the inception of this nation. They play a role
in healing the vulnerable and serving the community, and often they can help neighborhoods that are plagued by violence,
drugs, and poverty. They are inextricably linked to the con-
valescence of suffering communities. Through the program,
churches that offer drug counseling services or referrals and
transportation to drug treatment programs have become allies
in helping people heal.

Randy Burley, who spent over twenty years going in
and out of prison for selling drugs, became one of our most

passionate advocates. He set a wonderful example within one of our faith-based partnerships. I have spent countless hours talking to him to get a better understanding of the general state of young men I saw coming through the court. I consider him an expert because of his background. He has been on the front-lines doing gang interventions and reentry work with fathers. When I asked him what finally clicked for him to make him change his behavior, I was surprised by his answer.

"During my last prison stint, I noticed that the new admissions were getting younger and younger, and being admitted in greater numbers," he shared sadly. "I saw a nineteen-year-old boy with a fifty-year sentence. I could see that he was not built to handle it."

Mr. Burley spent his time in prison reflecting on his choices. "I used to tell myself that I don't sell drugs to children and pregnant women," he said about the moral boundaries he had set for himself. "But if I sold drugs to some people, and then they sold them to those same people, it was the same thing." He volunteered in prison, spending time in the library helping fellow inmates learn to read and write. He also devised a plan to make a larger contribution to the community that he had taken so much from.

When he got out of prison, he reconnected with a friend who attended New Hope Baptist Church, Whitney Houston's church. It had been running a soup kitchen for over fifty years, initially out of a tiny facility. The church eventually bought the building across the street to have more space to serve people. New Hope Now, the church's social service arm, has grown into a full-fledged organization that provides drug counseling, domestic violence counseling, job training and placement, financial support, and a reentry program that supports fathers by offering parental skills coaching and counseling (called Fathers on Fire)—all in addition to its long-standing soup kitchen.

After meeting with the minister, Mr. Burley began serving as an advocate for churchgoers' family members who had been caught in the criminal justice system or in the family court. He passionately fought to help keep families together, including advocating for parents who had completed drug rehabilitation and were trying to keep custody of their children. He showed up at the offices of child protective services so often to argue for his clients' rights that he was eventually banned from the building.

One day he ended up in my courtroom with a difficult participant. Recalling the experience, he said, "I saw something different than I saw in Hudson County, Essex County, and other courts. It was how you talked to people. You gave them simple rules. You gave them a choice, with respect. You were approachable, and you helped folks, or told them where to get help. That's why they were willing to surrender their feelings to you."

After witnessing this new approach at the Green Monster, he returned to the court with New Hope's deacon and lobbied for developing a partnership. He thought the church's social service organization could support the work of Newark Community Solutions. The church also invited defendants to volunteer with the soup kitchen, or simply to enjoy a meal.

Newark Community Solutions wrote an application on behalf of New Hope Now to Whole Foods Market's grant program. The organization was awarded the grant and received a new refrigeration system for the soup kitchen. Newark Community Solutions also received a supply of vegetable seeds. Court participants grew produce that was served in the soup kitchen.

Our institutions must mobilize one another and create initiatives to alleviate the social ills that lead to a life of crime. We must not let religious differences stalemate our efforts to save our communities. Faith-based institutions can initiate antiviolence programs, drug treatment counseling, and job training programs. They can serve as a stepping stone for people who are moving toward a better path, and they can support private businesses that later employ these citizens. These institutions exist to serve not only the individuals who attend their places of worship, but also others who are in their sphere of influence. And the sphere of influence must extend outside the doors of the house of worship.

This much is clear: if we do nothing, we lose our resources, the people. We need to come together to move forward as a nation. Spheres of influence can go well beyond faith communities. Moving people forward requires alliances between courts so that we are fashioning holistic resolutions. Defendants with mental health issues typically have cases in multiple jurisdictions, which means they regularly get picked up for unresolved cases. Many cases are charged as indictable offenses, which then get sent up to superior court at the state level. Convictions on those matters may result in prison sentences.

Some state-level courts are working on their own reforms and innovations to better serve communities on a larger scale. The superior court at Essex Vicinage piloted a diversionary program for offenders with a history of diagnosed mental illness. Defendants are offered a treatment program as an alternative to incarceration, or they are provided with treatment during incarceration.

Through Newark Community Solutions, the municipal court worked closely with the superior court's program to identify and manage defendants who had active cases in both courts and were admitted to both programs. Since the municipal court had a full cadre of social workers, we were often in a better position to monitor defendants and help them make appointments and get connected to services.

We also developed a close relationship with the US District Court of New Jersey's ReNew program. This federal reentry court serves defendants who are returning to their communities on parole after incarceration by providing them with services to help reduce recidivism. Upon completing the program, the individual is eligible to continue receiving services for up to one year while on parole and also to have time reduced on their parole. Many of these people enter prison with outstanding municipal fines, other open matters, or even traffic summonses. Through Newark Community Solutions, we scheduled them to appear in my court to manage their cases and give them time served for unresolved fines, and to dismiss old cases for the time spent in federal prison.

These coordinated efforts would not have been possible without Newark Community Solutions. We were able to extend services to community members through connections with other reform-minded courts. When we closed cases, we were able to break the yoke around the necks of people who had shouldered the burdens, most times for years, of unpaid fines, open warrants, and unresolved cases.

Newark Community Solutions' partnership with the court gave us countless opportunities to improve the delivery of justice. We may not be able to remedy the harm caused by years of senseless incarceration, the marginalizing of the poor, and the suffering of those struggling with past trauma, but we can begin to restore and repair individuals and their communities.

Critics may say that offering offenders a high level of support involves risk. But truly, the real risk comes when we continue to apply the same failed policies and practices that have brought us to this breaking point.

Chapter 6

TRANSFORMING
THE JUSTICE SYSTEM

To reduce the rate of incarceration and recidivism, and to improve public safety, we must think out of the box. Not only do the traditional practices fail to resolve problems communities face; their methods are often destructive, breaking families and communities further apart. Rather than deterring crime, the justice system seems stuck in methods that result in additional suffering and injustice. Injustice flourishes, and justice rapidly decays.

We have to chart a different path. We must invest in programs, initiatives, and projects that help us reverse the course on mass incarceration and counteract the justice system's inequitable effects on the poor and communities of color. Every institution within the justice system must assume additional responsibility to solve these problems. Many practitioners are working on reforms, and while nearly all initiatives have some value, I believe that focusing on three areas in particular will bring about the most significant shifts.

This chapter discusses my experience with youth court, violence-reduction programs, and procedural justice in policing, which I regard as the most promising methods to transform our criminal justice system.

Youth Court

The TV camera lights reflected off the diamond stud earring of the hefty teenager who occupied the chair behind the bench in Part One Criminal Court. The black robe he wore indicated that he was serving in the capacity of judge. During the day, this courtroom usually heard housing matters and served as conflict court, handling the city of Newark's employees' cases with an outside judge. Two evenings a week, the same space was converted into something rather different.

Tonight, it was bustling with high school students wearing green polo shirts that bore the white Newark Youth Court logo. They were preparing statements and questions for the impending case. The session was only slightly different from a usual youth court session, because *NBC Nightly News* was there to film the hearing. Although the pending case was of interest to producers, they were also there to capture the story of the young man serving as a judge in a room full of his peers.

An eighteen-year-old who was charged with assault took the stand. He'd had a fight with another teenager on a bus. Because of his age, he'd initially been charged as an adult. His case had landed in the municipal court but had been transferred to Newark Youth Court. The adults, namely the prosecutor and the public defender, wanted the defendant to find resolution among his teenage peers instead of being processed through the adult criminal system.

The members of the youth court's jury asked the defendant several questions about the incident and about himself. Then they deliberated. They made their decision, and the judge sentenced the young man to community service and attendance at workshops.

The judge had been a youth court participant himself. He had been expelled from school for making a threat. As a part of his sentence, he was required to sit on a youth court jury. After completing the program and being readmitted to school, he decided to apply to be a member of youth court. At the time of filming, he had plans to attend college in Pennsylvania.

The Newark Youth Court is a restorative justice program for young people aged ten to nineteen. Created in partnership with the Center for Court Innovation, and operated through Newark Community Solutions, it provides an alternative approach to the traditional methods of punishment of young people—one that is beneficial because its outcomes contrast starkly with the abysmal outcomes that result from conventional forms of student discipline. Youth court offers alternatives to school expulsion and to the adult criminal court system in an effort to keep young people in schools and in communities. It is an effective way to redirect them from the juvenile and adult criminal justice systems; early intervention can help young people steer clear of entrapment in the prison system.

Young people who appear before youth court are called respondents. The jurors, called members, are other city teens. Members decide the most equitable consequence for the respondent's "offense." All the youth court practitioners are teenagers from local public, private, or charter high schools; they make up a true jury of the respondent's peers. Even though youth court serves as a diversionary and early-intervention program, it also develops leadership skills in its members. It uses positive peer pressure to change the behavior of members' peers.

Newark Youth Court receives referrals from schools, the police department, the law department, family court, the department of probation, and even from parents who need assistance with their children's behavior. It reports to the referring agency on a respondent's compliance or noncompliance. Consequences for noncompliance lie solely with the referring agency, not with the youth court. Although accepting referrals from various agencies can have a tremendous impact on the diversion of young people from the justice system, partnerships with schools prove particularly beneficial.

As a reaction to the school shootings that increased in number in the 1990s, US school districts began instituting zero-tolerance policies for in-school infractions. These policies also proliferated under the popular but wrongheaded "broken windows" theory of policing, which argues that maintaining order by aggressively policing low-level offenses prevents more serious crimes. There was little evidence that it worked as intended in areas where it was implemented. Instead, it resulted in extreme overpolicing of Black and Brown communities, further fracturing the relationship between law enforcement and people of color.[1]

Similarly, zero-tolerance policies, which impose extremely punitive penalties, began diverting young people from school through suspensions and expulsions, often ultimately landing them in jail and prison. This progression has become known as the school-to-prison pipeline.

It's important to note that these funnels affect girls and young women differently than they do boys and young men. As described in an earlier chapter, young women are more susceptible to the "sexual abuse to prison pipeline," defined as a causal connection between being a victim of sexual abuse and the commission of offenses such as truancy, fighting, illicit drugs, and running away. These behaviors, which relate to unaddressed trauma, lead to suspension from school and subsequent entry into the juvenile and adult criminal justice systems.[2]

A comprehensive study of school discipline conducted by the Center for Court Innovation reviewed over eight hundred New York City schools. It confirmed biased and disparate discipline, finding that Black and Hispanic students, male students, students with disabilities, and low-income students were more likely to be suspended than other students with similar past behavior. Findings also showed that Black students received harsher school suspensions than other students. In schools with high suspension rates and a large number of Black and Hispanic students, those students were found to be significantly more likely to have a future arrest. Yet the study's results also showed that the use of restorative justice practices, peace circles, and restorative conversations such as staff-led mediations led to an increased sense of physical and emotional safety for students.[3]

Many of the Newark Youth Court cases referred through schools are for truancy, theft, school vandalism, fighting, trespassing, harassment, and occasionally marijuana possession. Disciplinary actions for these infractions usually result in detention or harsher penalties. By sending cases to youth court instead, the school decides to rely on the court's sanctions and to refrain from suspension or expulsion. The student receives an intervention while still being able to continue their education, which can be vital in keeping them out of poverty and the court system later in life.

The leadership component of youth court trains young people about the legal process and how to serve as courtroom actors: jurors, judges, and community and youth advocates. They are also trained in restorative justice principles, and in how to respond to harmful behavior they may encounter. The theory of restorative justice proposes that when someone commits a crime, a tear is created in the community's relationships. Restorative justice emphasizes more than retribution against the offender. It provides broader options for dealing with wrongdoings, specifically repairing harm caused by the act. It offers all parties an opportunity for healing. Howard Zehr, a highly regarded authority on restorative justice, describes the practice as "a process to involve, to the extent possible, those who have a stake in a specific offense and to collectively identify and address harms, needs, and obligations, in order to heal and put things as right as possible."[4] This approach assists respondents in understanding the consequences of their behavior and helps them to make amends.

Youth court referrals from the Newark Police Department are called stationhouse adjustments. The stationhouse adjustment program intends to provide immediate consequences—from community service to restitution to resolution for the victim—while helping the teen avoid the stigma of a formal juvenile delinquency record. When an officer considers a young person's offense, the officer can decide to forgo filing a juvenile criminal complaint. This can be done on a range of incidents, from low-level offenses to felony crimes—for example, theft, shoplifting, disorderly conduct, trespassing, or criminal mischief (the defacing or destruction of property).

Consider the case of a ten-year-old playing outdoors. The child throws stones at a satellite dish, damaging it. Unfortunately for the child, the satellite dish is the property of the Newark Police Department. The police take him into custody. However, instead of charging him with criminal mischief and putting him through the juvenile justice system, they elect to give him a stationhouse adjustment. He is referred to the Newark Youth Court. The coordinator screens his case for appropriateness and calls his mother for consent. The boy receives a hearing date. Because the process is based on the concept of restorative justice, he must accept responsibility for his action in this instance. In a significant departure from how the traditional justice system operates, Newark Youth Court members do not determine the guilt or innocence of the respondent. He must acknowledge that he committed the wrongdoing and that it caused a harm.

The case is assigned to a community advocate and a respondent advocate. The boy meets with the respondent advocate, his representative, in the hallway before the hearing. When the hearing begins and the teen judge calls the case, he is escorted into court by the teen bailiff as his mother takes a seat in the front row.

The community advocate speaks first and makes a case before the jurors for a sanction that appropriately addresses the harm the boy's behavior caused. The respondent advocate acknowledges their client's conduct but points out his positive attributes while pleading for leniency.

The healing begins when the teen jurors ask the respondent questions about the incident. They also ask him about himself: how he spends his days, whether he thinks he needs a role model. The jurors head into the judge's chambers to deliberate and later return with a sanction that is based in part on the respondent's answers to their questions. In this case, the sanctions include community service and workshops. What is most powerful about the sanctions is that respondents perform them alongside other youth court participants.

Addressing the school-to-prison pipeline is critical if we are serious about ending mass incarceration. School should be seen as a place that prepares our young people for higher education and for becoming productive members of society. Unfortunately, too often school functions as a funnel, delivering our children into the prison-industrial complex because of ill-conceived policies. Widely implementing youth courts could offer broad positive impacts for current and future generations. As in many other aspects of life, prevention is the most effective—and least costly—remedy.

Violence-Reduction Programs

Two outreach workers at Newark United Against Violence (NUAV) had devised a plan. It was Middy Brown's idea, and it seemed insane. But Demitrius Carol, Mr. Brown's friend, colleague, and mentee, trusted him, so he went along with it. Their objective was to reduce violence throughout the city of Newark by getting to the individuals in the middle of it and offering them jobs and services. The pair had decided they would approach their longtime nemesis, a rival gang leader, to suggest that he come down to the office and sign up for the work program. For Mr. Brown and Mr. Carol, both former gang members, this was dangerous. The OG they wanted to speak to had been released from federal prison seven days prior and would likely soon resume making the poor decisions that had gotten him sent in.

Fights among rival gangs for territory had been tearing up the neighborhoods for decades. "The beef started way before any of us even was born," said Mr. Carol. He had a sense of what they were up against and was still in disbelief that he had let Mr. Brown talk him into this. Mr. Brown said, "I was reading *The 48 Laws of Power*, and the second principle said don't put too much faith in your friends, and learn how to use your enemies. This beef was so old that we didn't even know what it was about. People feel a particular way about a thing and never talk about it."

Mr. Brown, now an actor and instructor, had decided to change his life after federal law enforcement agents, while searching for him, had burst into his mother's home, dragged her out of bed nude, zip-tied her hands, and had her kneel next to his sister as officers held guns to their heads.

The two men hopped into Mr. Brown's car and went out to find the OG to offer their services. "We told him, 'We have a plan for you. Just come to the office, and we can help you stay off this corner,'" Mr. Brown recounted.

But the OG would have no part of their plan.

Doggedly persistent, Mr. Brown decided they would go to his house every day until they convinced him. For two weeks, they appeared at his house, offering him assistance and trying to put the beef behind them.

One afternoon, as Mr. Brown and Mr. Carol sat in the office of NUAV, the OG walked in with ten other gang members to sign up for the work program. Not only had the two outreach workers cajoled the OG into accepting assistance, but he had brought his followers, which legitimized the program and opened the door for others to join.

This story demonstrates the effectiveness of the "credible messenger" in efforts to reduce violence. These individuals' street cred, life experiences, and accounts of personal redemption are compelling tools for attempting to reach people involved in the justice system and helping them transform their lives. Also known as violence interrupters, they effectively engage individuals who are entangled in gang and criminal activity. Having been involved in the justice system themselves, they convey credibility when they share their stories and the message of change.

Former gang leaders and formerly incarcerated people should not be cast aside but rather enlisted in this work of healing the community. But they need to be provided with the skills to do so. Mr. Carol is a prime example of an effective credible messenger. An African American man in his thirties, he became involved with the criminal justice system at age thirteen, about the time that his mom became drug addicted and left him to fend for himself. He served ten years in prison for robbery and carjacking. Upon being granted parole, like others from Newark he was advised that he could not be paroled to any address within that city. This meant he could not go to the residence of any family member who lived in Newark. Instead, he was sent to a homeless shelter.

Once there, Mr. Carol reached out to the city's reentry case manager, Kareem Motley, who in turn connected him to Newark Community Solutions' social worker, Sienna Hunter-Cuyjet. They were able to get him out of the shelter, enrolled in community college, and subsequently enrolled in the city's partnership with the Greater Newark Conservancy's Clean and Green Program. This program provides on-the-job training in landscaping to justice-system-involved and formerly incarcerated residents. Due to Mr. Carol's progress in the program and in school, he was asked to serve as one of the first outreach workers at Newark United Against Violence.

Mr. Carol felt like a hypocrite lecturing young men about doing things he had done himself, so he used different recruitment tactics. He employed a "show and tell" strategy by bringing up an event in the community. He might say to a potential recruit, "Hey, man, did you hear what happened to JoJo?"

"Yeah, they shot him right in the middle of the day."

Mr. Carol would reply, "Yeah, if he was working or at school, JoJo wouldn't have been outside to get shot."

After convincing someone to come to the office, he would enroll them in Clean and Green, teach them how to complete job applications, help them with their resume, and conduct mock interviews. Participants received a $500 bonus if they obtained permanent employment after completing the program. This made getting a job competitive.

"What was wonderful is that they didn't even realize they were developing as they were going through the process of learning how to fill out applications and what to say during interviews," Mr. Carol told me. "They'd come back from interviews and tell the counselor and the outreach workers, 'This part didn't go well, so when I go back, I'm gonna do it like this.'"

Now a supervisor at a growing national company, Mr. Carol still sets aside time to assist young men who are interested in making a change. He partners with small businesses that need laborers and connects them to men who are willing to work, and he continues to help young men write resumes and prepare for interviews.

Clean and Green was one of the programs offered by Hotspots, a violence-reduction project that began in Newark.

It was managed in part by the city's Office of Reentry and funded by a grant from the US Department of Justice's Office of Juvenile Justice and Delinquency Prevention. Newark Community Solutions operated Hotspots from an office in the community—located in a hotspot. Hotspots borrowed from Ceasefire programs in Boston, which focused on law enforcement involvement, and Chicago, which relied on significant outreach to potential participants and included the delivery of social services. Hotspots emphasized prevention. Using the police department's crime-mapping data, Hotspots concentrated its efforts in areas of Newark that had high rates of homicides and shootings. The program recruited Newark residents who were between eighteen and thirty and were at high risk of becoming victims or perpetrators of violence.

Program workers drilled into participants the message of living a better life, free of violence and justice system involvement. A wide range of wraparound services was offered to participants: talk therapy, food assistance, identification, educational services, and governmental assistance. As a transitional jobs program, Clean and Green provided temporary work to help participants develop skills and obtain experience and references. It provided thirteen weeks of employment, paying eight dollars per hour for up to thirty-two hours a week. Participants were trained in landscaping and horticulture, and they cleaned and beautified the city while also maintaining an urban farm.

I was always surprised by the individuals who stopped selling drugs to take a relatively low-paying job. Many of them said it was better than having to look over their shoulder for the cops, or for someone trying to shoot them to get their spot on a corner. For most, the program afforded the only opportunity to obtain legitimate work.

Utilizing a broad range of expertise, and exemplifying the advantages of partnership, Hotspots benefited from the Newark Violence Reduction Initiative (NVRI), which worked in partnership with the Newark Police Department, Rutgers University School of Criminal Justice, and the Center for Crime Prevention and Control at John Jay College of Criminal Justice.

Newark Community Solutions also provided participants with individual and group counseling. First, a licensed social worker conducted psychological screenings and assessments for program candidates. Admitted participants were required to engage in cognitive behavioral therapy (CBT), defined by the American Psychological Association as a psychotherapeutic approach that addresses dysfunctional emotions, behaviors, and cognitions through setting goals.[5] CBT, a form of talk therapy, has been successful in the treatment of anxiety, substance abuse, and psychotic disorders. It helps individuals better manage decision-making by adjusting behavioral and thought processes, ideally leading to an improved quality of life. It teaches participants how to shift their decisions around engaging in violence. The program counselors also employ applied behavior analysis, or ABA, which uses the theory of behaviorism to modify human behavior as part of a learning or treatment process.[6]

Newark Community Solutions' overarching goal was to provide participants with transitional work, assist them in dealing with the trauma they had experienced, and give them tools to create lasting life change. The program workers provided services to everyone who approached them, even those who could not receive a transitional job because of funding limitations. Case managers and outreach workers assisted clients in obtaining public benefits, resolving outstanding warrants, meeting child support obligations, addressing substance abuse issues, and taking on mental and physical health needs.

As mentioned earlier in the chapter, one of the most effective aspects of this program was the use of credible messengers for its outreach services. Credible messengers aim to motivate participants to shift away from negative and dangerous thinking and decision-making. They accomplish this by fostering trusting relationships with the individuals and their families. Equally important, credible messengers can legitimize the program for potential candidates based on their past reputations. Recent research suggests that survivors of violence who are paired with a violence-intervention mentor have low recidivism rates.[7]

Hotspots outreach workers were actively engaged in participants' day-to-day lives, serving as a reminder of their commitment to a new lifestyle. They supported participants in everything from finding and keeping permanent, full-time employment to renegotiating a vision of a life without crime. They helped organize alternative weekend activities for participants who needed to change their exposure to people, places, and things. They traveled with them to job interviews and court appointments. As we know, navigating these systems can be demoralizing. Having support can help individuals overcome the barriers they face. Outreach workers also provided a "rapid response" following a homicide or shooting—for example, visiting the family of the victim in the hospital emergency department or in the family's home.

Participants in Hotspots receive referrals to victim support services, which is critical because they are often themselves victims of violence. These services are extended to families and friends so that even those peripherally affected by the trauma of violence can receive therapy and care.

The services offered by Hotspots were invaluable for defendants who came through my court but were not eligible for the Newark Community Solutions program. It afforded me an alternative space where I could send high-risk individuals, like Sam Salaam.

He likes to put his hands on women, but he can't look me in the eye, I thought when I called his case. He was in court for domestic violence. Mr. Salaam wore his dreadlocks in a half ponytail, the longer dreads resting on his shoulders. He stood with his shoulders slumped and his hands clasped behind his back. After his handcuffs were removed, he still looked defeated, like he was facing the inevitable.

Mr. Salaam had four domestic violence files, and four women were standing by the prosecutor's desk. When I asked if they were family members, the prosecutor indicated that they were the complaining witnesses on the files—that is, the alleged victims. They all began to shout at once, saying some variation on "I just want to dismiss my case." The court had already adjudicated some cases, so Mr. Salaam had pled guilty.

Right then, I had an epiphany: *We've been approaching these cases wrong. There will never be a shortage of victims.*

Mr. Salaam had been sentenced to six months in jail and had been required to attend a judicially monitored batterer's-intervention therapy, which he had failed to complete. He had also failed to appear before the sentencing judge to give him an update. This had led to the issuance of a bench warrant and his arrest.

The judge who had imposed the initial sentence was no longer serving as a judge. I held Mr. Salaam to bail for being a flight risk and for also having open cases. He went to the county jail. For domestic violence cases, judges are trained to punish the aggressor and to avoid significantly revictimizing the survivor.

The courts are terrified of these cases. We can't predict the continuing level of violence, and too many cases result in homicide. However, I knew that merely punishing the aggressor was usually inadequate. I recalled a sermon by T. D. Jakes of the Potter's House in which he talked about counseling men who had committed domestic violence. Reverend Jakes shared that he had never counseled a batterer who felt good about himself.

Armed with this realization, I saw that we needed to change the aggressor, to improve them. If we could adjust how they felt about themselves, then maybe we could help them alter their violent behavior. With much trepidation, I decided to set aside my fear and delve into Mr. Salaam's case. His victims deserved better. I thought about the many times I'd had to kick a victim on a domestic violence case out of court and into the hallway for screaming at me, giving me an attitude, or disrupting court because I wouldn't dismiss a case against their alleged batterer. I understood that the victim often wanted to protect the batterer out of fear or love; this didn't make me feel better about their situation.

When Mr. Salaam appeared in court via video from the jail, I started my interrogation. I looked at the TV screen and noticed that he had a little boy's face even though he was almost thirty. I asked, "Do you have any children?"

He looked surprised by the question. He hesitantly responded, "Yeah . . . two boys and a girl."

"What will you say when your daughter tells you her husband or boyfriend is putting his hands on her?"

He puffed up and responded, "I'm going to jail . . ."

I interjected and said, "No, you're not. She's not even going to tell you if someone is abusing her, because you are teaching your daughter how men should treat her by how you treat her mom."

He lowered his eyes. After a protracted silence, he touched the corner of his eye as if to wipe away a tear.

"Don't you want better for your children? Isn't that the minimum you're supposed to give them? A better life than you had. Do you have a high school diploma?"

Eyes still lowered, he said, "No."

"Well, how are you going to give them better, and you don't even have a diploma?" I said, giving him a reflective pause as I waited for a response. No answer.

"We have a program down here at the courthouse, and they can get you into a GED program. I want to put a hold on the counseling sessions and see if we can get you some help first. Are you interested in that?"

I held off on the anger-management counseling because his record told me that he had already been sentenced to it, and it had done nothing. I believed if we could build his confidence, he might be less likely to engage in partner violence.

"I am, Judge," he responded enthusiastically, realizing I was going to release him.

"You do understand that if I release you, like the last judge did, and you don't return, I'm going to smoke you. There's no conversation, no explanation. You are going to go to jail every time I see you." I explained myself clearly. "There's no ROR [release on your own recognizance] for you after this. I'm going to send the fugitive squad to your house to pick you up. And you know I don't forget a conversation or a face. And you better not pick up one more domestic violence case while you are out on my ROR. You are out on Judge Pratt's time. Now you can try me if you like. I wouldn't."

"Judge, I know. You don't play," he said as if he had read it on a bathroom wall. I was going to take a chance on him to help restore this family, but he needed to understand, in no uncertain terms, that there would be repercussions for failing to do his part.

A few days later, before his court date, Mr. Salaam was sitting in the courtroom. Officer Carillo approached the bench and said, "He says you told him to come see you?"

As he swaggered to counsel's table, I recognized the baby face. "Sir, you don't have court today. What are you doing here?"

"Judge, you told me to come holler at you if I wanted help getting my GED," he reminded me.

"Well, I'm certain I never told anyone to come holler at me," I retorted as the courtroom burst into laughter. I believe he was testing me. He wanted to show me he was serious, but he also wanted to see if I would do what I said I would do.

Instead of reassigning the batterer's-intervention treatment, I decided to monitor him through Newark Community Solutions. That way, I could control the quality of counseling, get frequent reports, and perform close monitoring. It also meant that I had a more comprehensive array of services to offer him, and I could be on the lookout for potential victims.

This is something frowned upon in traditional courts. There, judges either sentence batterers to jail, order them to attend anger management, or send them to batterer's intervention, which is typically done as a group and seen as an escalation in counseling. Batterers are given a list of places that offer counseling, which includes faith-based institutions. They are rescheduled to appear in court to report on their progress. Upon the completion of counseling, their cases are dismissed.

My approach, however, would be more holistic, holding Mr. Salaam accountable the entire way.

Due to the nature of his cases, he wasn't eligible to formally participate in the Newark Community Solutions program. However, like any other person in the community, he was eligible to receive services as a walk-in. Most importantly, he was eligible for the Hotspots program, through which he would receive counseling from a licensed social worker and through group meetings. The clinic also referred him to an educational program where he would receive a high school diploma upon successfully passing the GED exam.

On his review date, I asked him about the GED class, and he said, "It's alright."

I pressed further. "No, I mean, what are you learning?"

Counting on his fingers, he said, "I'm learning whole numbers, fractions, and algebra." And then he paused and said, "And Judge, for the first time, I was able to help my son with his homework, because he's learning fractions. I always have to push him off on his mom because I don't know."

"And how did that make you feel?"

"Like a man, Judge," he answered. Applause came from a man sitting in the back of the courtroom. We all joined in. I realized that countless incidents occurred each day that reminded Mr. Salaam of his diminished manhood. I always focused on the most obvious issues for the Black and Brown men who came through the courtroom: the lack of gainful employment, or how a criminal charge would prevent employers from hiring them. However, it had never dawned on me that the lack of an appropriate education added to feelings of unworthiness.

Weeks later Mr. Salaam appeared in court unscheduled. Once again, the officer informed me that he wanted to speak to me. He popped his collar and swaggered down the aisle as if he were the next contestant on *The Price Is Right*. It had been a lengthy court session, so I appreciated the entertainment. When he arrived at counsel's table, he handed the officer an envelope to give to me.

I opened the envelope, and it contained a high school diploma from the state of New Jersey with his name on it. He had passed the GED exam. He shared that he had received numerous congratulatory comments on Facebook after posting about his newly acquired diploma. His was the first of many such diplomas that I would receive from defendants. At his final court appearance, I praised his compliance with treatment, congratulated him on completing the program, and vacated his fines.

Long after he had completed his time with the court, I heard, "Hey, Judge Pratt!" Still looking youthful, Mr. Salaam wore a dirty Newark Conservancy T-shirt and boots. He had received a job through the Clean and Green program and was reporting to his case manager. He had also obtained a job working for a sanitation company during the graveyard shift. He had had another argument with his girlfriend that landed him in court. There was no physical violence, however, and she never appeared in court on the matter. A year later, he reappeared in court on a marijuana charge that was adjudicated.

Mr. Salaam was not a perfect defendant, but he was significantly improved. His and his family's lives had been elevated due to his achievements through the courts and the violence-reduction program. Jail hadn't altered his behavior. His involvement with the Hotspots program had provided the impetus for slow, methodical change. By helping batterers modify their behavior, we serve their victims.

A traditional court, which relies on conventional counseling from various sources, some nonclinical, for domestic violence cases, has fewer options. Such cases, however, require multilevel interventions for both defendants and victims. Merely hoping and praying that there will be no escalation in violence is insufficient. In this instance, the defendant feared and respected the judge, and he was given access to services, education, mentorship, and support.

Another unforeseen benefit of the violence-reduction program is that it brings together the most unlikely foes. One spring day, weeks after Mr. Salaam had completed his mandates with the court, a group of five men wearing safety vests and dirt-stained Newark Conservancy T-shirts entered the muggy courtroom. After stumbling around, they settled into the back row. This was particularly odd for the middle of a session. Officer Carillo approached the bench to tell me they would like to speak to me. I thought, *What kind of foolishness is going on today? A busy court day, and all of a sudden I have visitors.*

I invited them forward. They walked with no apprehension, anger, or annoyance—the emotions I typically see when people approach the bench. They stood shoulder to shoulder behind counsel's table with the positive energy of young men who are joking around. I recognized some of them, including Mr. Salaam.

The spokesman for the group, almost blushing, said, "We came by here to invite you to our Clean and Green graduation, Judge." My heart warmed. Their supervisor stood in the back of the courtroom with his arms crossed, beaming with pride. "It would mean a lot to us if you could come," the spokesman said.

"Well, tell the people in court here what this Clean and Green is about," I said.

Interrupting each other, they began to explain. One of them said, "We all from different gangs, different sects, and neighborhoods, and we all friends now. . . ."

Another young man said, "No, man, we brothers."

The other men nodded their heads and shook hands in response to this correction. Were my eyes and ears conspiring to deceive me?

The young man continued, "We working together when we go into different neighborhoods, and we tell folks, 'They with us, just let him through.' We even hang out together on the weekends."

These men, many of whom were expected to shoot each other on sight, were learning to resolve their differences. Being part of a violence-reduction program and getting to know one another was helping them put an end to their hostilities. The benefits of focusing our energy on addressing the sources of violent crimes are innumerable.

Procedural Justice in Policing

"Judge, let me tell you what recently happened," Jon Henriquez, a veteran officer on the police force and a Portuguese American from Newark, said excitedly. Known for his calm demeanor, he was one of the officers working in the Deuce when I began. He was later promoted to sergeant and became responsible for training new officers, including those in the juvenile unit. One day, as he was patrolling an area near a liquor store with the trainees, an older African American man standing in front of the store said to him, "Hey, Mr. Question Man. I got a question for you now. If you get it wrong, you got to give me a dollar."

The guy had reversed the whole game on him. Sergeant Henriquez replied, "I'm not doing that anymore," and they shared a hearty laugh.

As the guy walked away, a rookie officer asked, "What was that about?"

Sergeant Henriquez explained that in my court he was responsible for the people in custody waiting to see the judge. While they waited, he would play Jailhouse Jeopardy with them: an assortment of effortless questions about current events. He rewarded correct answers with doughnuts he purchased each morning. (Yes, doughnuts.) The others he would give away.

He said to me, "I told the officers it was a win–win situation. The game entertained the defendants as they waited to have their cases heard, so they weren't disruptive, and they got to know me. Now when they see me in the community, there is no hostility."

Deciding to use his exchange outside the liquor store as a teaching moment, Sergeant Henriquez told the trainees, "You will deal with a lot of people out here. You won't remember them all, but they will never forget you. Treating people with respect is how you build trust in the community. If there was an incident in this area, I could have used that interaction to get information, even turned him into a confidential informant.

These folks never stray far from where you find them. This is how you get information to close out cases."

He explained to me, "This story resonated with them. Judge, when you first started in court, I thought it was crazy that you were just going to let these folks go after we arrested them." He referred to the newly implemented police training programs Trauma to Trust, Equal Justice USA, Resilient Justice, and Peer to Peer. "I was bragging about how Judge Pratt was doing all this stuff for years. She told us that this was where the future of criminal justice was headed."

This story affirms the residual power of ensuring that people maintain their dignity during interactions with the justice system, including with police. Sergeant Henriquez was able to demonstrate to rookie officers that change is possible through training. What follows in this section is the most effective strategy for improving police and community relations.

Marches, protests, and violence: these are the outraged responses to our distrusted police system, and they suggest that the system is imploding. Complaints of police abuses of authority—through the brutalizing, disrespecting, and harassing of civilians—are persistent. Ignoring the voices of the disillusioned is a formula for ongoing battles in our communities. Whether community members report crimes and cooperate with officers during investigations depends on whether they trust and have confidence in the officers who are policing their communities.

Nowhere is this lack of confidence in the police greater than in communities of color. A 2016 Pew Research report titled *The Racial Confidence Gap in Police Performance* showed that Blacks were about half as likely as whites to have a favorable view of policing in their community. Specifically, only 33 percent of Black people surveyed believed that officers were using the right amount of force for each situation, as opposed to 75 percent of white people. Regarding officer misconduct, merely 31 percent of Blacks believed that officers were held accountable when misconduct occurred, compared to 70 percent of whites. Staggeringly, only 14 percent of Blacks had a lot of confidence in their community's police.[8]

These statistics show why implementing a process like procedural justice in policing is imperative: it improves community-police relations with minimum effort.

The article "Procedural Justice: A Training Model for Organizational-Level Change," which appeared online in *Police Chief Magazine*, lays out precisely how law enforcement organizations should employ procedural justice. A collaboration between the US Department of Justice's COPS Office and the University of Illinois at Chicago's Center for Public Safety and Justice developed a multitiered training initiative that works to insert procedural justice into organizational culture. The pilot project trained 4,135 people involved in law enforcement, including civilian employees and community members.

The model relies on the central pillars of procedural justice, namely fairness, transparency, voice, and impartiality. These values must become commonplace within law enforcement organizations. Researchers found that the effectiveness and success of the model in changing the culture depended on conducting training at the executive, supervisor, frontline, and community levels. The first step begins with trainers engaging in a "Conversation with the Chief" to assess readiness and ensure support for the program at the level of top leadership.[9]

A constant theme of effective police training in procedural justice is the need for supervisors to be committed to practicing the principles internally with staff as well as externally with the community. Officers need to perceive that they are treated with dignity, respect, and fairness by their supervisors and co-workers. Poor treatment can result in officers projecting that behavior on the individuals whom they are meant to serve. For law enforcement leadership, the proverbial notion to practice what you preach is indispensable when promoting a more procedurally just culture.

External procedural justice refers to the methods, procedures, and activities developed by police departments to aid officers in building trust and rapport with the community. This includes introducing new language and processes for engagement. When responding to a situation, officers need to consider how they speak to community members as well as the attitude they project. In the initial training, frontline officers were instructed on the application of procedural justice in their daily interactions. Incorporating restorative practices (more on this below), they were trained to engage community members in a manner that promoted open communication. This gave community members voice by allowing them to be heard, especially their complaints.[10]

The report mentions that another important factor in improving relations is police participating in or hosting community activities that are not centered on law enforcement. Captain Rasheen Peppers, a veteran of the Newark Police Department, builds public trust by hosting the Captain's Corner in the 5th Precinct. This event brings together medical and social service providers, staff of city agencies such as welfare and housing, and employees from local and national businesses such as Home Depot, FedEx, and Popeyes, who guarantee jobs to individuals, including those with records. The gatherings, which are held in different locations within the 5th Precinct's area, bring resources to the residents while also offering fun activities for children. They are resident-focused family and community events.

The authors of an article titled "Representative Bureaucracy in Policing: Does It Increase Perceived Legitimacy?" explain that female officers positively influence the perception of law enforcement, including a police force's job performance, trustworthiness, and fairness—traits essential to procedural justice.[11] According to a 2021 study of the Chicago Police Department, women officers of all races used less force with civilians than their white male counterparts. Most significantly, the study found that Black, Hispanic, and women officers made fewer stops, made fewer arrests for minor violations, and used less force against civilians than their white male colleagues. These findings support the benefits of diversifying police forces.[12]

They also corroborate an earlier study indicating that, in comparison to their male counterparts, female officers were less likely to be named in citizen complaints, as well as less likely to be subject to allegations of excessive force. The research further indicated that female officers' presence led to more success in defusing violent or aggressive behavior, which explained the reduction of force used by officers when a female officer was present.[13]

This is not to say that women are "naturally" peaceful, nor that men are "naturally" violent. Women are generally socialized to be more communal and caregiving, while men are generally socialized to be aggressive and dominant. A lifetime of such socialization and its ensuing rewards leads to ingrained habits and attitudes.

A goal of procedural justice in policing is to prevent difficult circumstances, like use of force, and evidence suggests that female officers tend to be inclined toward such tactics. Unfortunately, according to the Women's Leadership Academy, an organization that seeks to train, recruit, promote, and advocate for women in law enforcement, women make up just 12 percent of police officers.[14] Despite this underwhelming statistic, the benefits of having women in policing are invaluable.

***

Traditional police training does not promote procedural justice tactics. To paraphrase the title of an article by journalist Alana Semuels, American society pays the price for outdated police training methods. A shortage of law enforcement officers results in the need to enroll as many individuals as possible in police academies, potentially perpetuating problems—from a failure to identify problematic cadets, to a drastic difference in policing methods across the country, to a lack of formal oversight during training.[15]

Randy Shrewsberry, founder of the Institute for Criminal Justice Training Reform, seeks to reimagine police training for these very reasons. He asserts that many police-related incidents, like shootings and excessive use of force, are directly linked to a series of training failures, from inadequate time spent educating cadets to militarized "Warrior Cop"–style instruction.[16] It is evident that police training needs a new, innovative approach, which can be found with procedural justice.

Procedural justice is not fail proof. In the article "Rebuilding Trust Between Police and Community Through Procedural Justice and Reconciliation," the authors advise, "One drawback of the procedural justice approach is that its lack of attention to [events of] the past means that any existing distrust can slow the process of trust-building, with community members interpreting their new experiences through the lens of the past."[17] Police departments can overcome this shortcoming by pairing procedural justice with reconciliation, which restores relationships by requiring law enforcement agents to perform gestures designed to earn the trust of skeptical communities. These gestures address the community rather than individuals, and they acknowledge both historical and present-day reasons for distrust.

To change feelings of distrust between police and the Black, Latinx, and other marginalized communities they serve, officers' interactions with these groups must change. More precisely, community members must believe they are safe from police-inflicted force and violence. The Newark Police Department reported that in 2020, there were no police-initiated shootings in the city, despite a nationwide spike in homicides and violent crime during COVID-19 and after quarantine.[18] De-escalation training has been credited for this result. The authors of the report *Principles of Procedurally Just Policing*, from Yale University's Justice Collaboratory, stress, "Yet another benefit of de-escalation is that many de-escalation tools are also aligned with treating individuals with respect and slowing situations down enough for the officer to listen to and communicate productively with the individual."[19] Further, according to a report from the US Department of Justice, "From procedural justice research, we know that these actions improve public perception of the police department."[20] De-escalation responses are centered on communication tactics that are consistent with procedural justice.

In an interview in which we discussed de-escalation tactics, Captain Rasheen Peppers described to me how during a ride with a new officer, they encountered a woman who was illegally double-parked. The new officer noticed that she had a child in the vehicle. In an attempt to give her a citation, he asked her to lower her window. She refused. The new officer told her that he would have to remove her from the vehicle if she did not comply. Captain Peppers, not wanting the incident to become physical, surveyed the neighborhood and saw a young man sitting on a porch nearby. He approached the man and asked if he knew the woman in the car. The young man said yes, and the captain asked if he would talk to her. He obliged.

To help the woman maintain her dignity in front of the child and to avoid scaring the boy, the officers placed a neighbor between themselves and the woman. They ran her plates and issued her two summonses. And that was the end of the traffic stop. They extended their de-escalation tactics not only to the subject of the parking violation, but also to the member of the community who was recruited to intervene. A simple run of the plates got them the desired results. Employing de-escalation techniques requires a fundamental shift in police behavior and a constant check of the ego. These techniques must be the new normal.

For law enforcement, earning the community's trust is essential. As I've stated throughout this book, distrust of the criminal justice system continues to be a severe problem. Police agencies have been the enforcers of segregation and racial discrimination toward communities of color for generations. Procedural justice and reconciliation can help officers alter their behavior toward the communities they serve and thus gain their confidence. For these concepts to work, the people and institutions in authority must change from an attitude of merely expecting the individuals they come in contact with to bend to their will. In essence, the research recommends that law enforcement agencies (1) shift to a service model from the traditional military model, and (2) evaluate the community's reception of their sincere gestures and adjust as needed.

There are several advantages to both procedural justice and reconciliation. Procedural justice uses respectful and un-biased dispute-settling tactics; reconciliation focuses on gestures intended to earn trust. Procedural justice is inherently individualistic, promoting trust through positive and fair interpersonal interactions; reconciliation is intrinsically community centered, addressing the entire community and acknowledging past wrongs. When these practices are combined, they profoundly impact community-police relations, particularly in reinstating credibility.[21]

Failure to infuse a procedural justice approach into policing will continue to produce terrible outcomes throughout the justice system, as was the case for David Polyneice. The young man stood before me, scowling. I had noticed his furled eyebrows and creased forehead when he sat in the audience. When I called his name, he rolled his eyes, placed his hands on the seat before him, heaved his svelte frame to standing, and walked toward counsel's table as if he were about to fight. Because I didn't recognize him from previous court appearances, I surmised that his rage came from his contact with the police. I see it multiple times a day. I thought, *Oh boy, must have been a pretty bad interaction.* I warned him with the "not today" look.

The prosecutor and public defender asked to approach the bench. They explained that his case had been transferred from another court. Mr. Polyneice was a law student who, while hanging out with a friend, had had an encounter with the transit police. He'd been charged with being a disorderly person on a quality-of-life ticket. It was clear that this particular case irritated the prosecutor. She considered the incident to be minor; it did not deserve to rise to the level of a disorderly persons offense. I assigned Mr. Polyneice an essay and had him meet with the social worker in the event he needed assistance.

The incident that led to Mr. Polyneice's appearance in my court occurred while he and a friend were waiting for a city train. His friend, unable to hold it anymore, decided to urinate in the dark in an alcove at the subway stop. A New Jersey Transit Police officer appeared and began to berate the friend, cursing and calling him an animal, among other insults. Mr. Polyneice, the law student, intervened by telling the officer that while he had the right to give his friend a summons, he didn't have a right to insult him. The officer turned toward Mr. Polyneice, body-slammed him, and charged him with disorderly persons. As Mr. Polyneice put it, the officer shoved his face into the concrete "just for speaking up for a friend."

Fortunately for Mr. Polyneice, the prosecutors in both courts felt a deep sense of sympathy toward him and were also willing to look beyond the allegation scribbled on the quality-of-life summons. Unaware of the police officer's actions, I assigned an essay. Later, I dismissed his case, and he returned to his life. Although Mr. Polyneice could have lodged a complaint against the officer, he, like so many others, did not. The officer experienced no retribution for his actions, but Mr. Polyneice was left to deal with the indignity done to him.

Years later, while attending a legal event, I was approached by a young, sharply dressed African American man who extended his hand and said, "I don't know if you remember me, but I want to say thank you." Mr. Polyneice, the former snarling defendant, now standing before me in full attorney regalia, was an assistant attorney general. I could barely contain my joy. Before our conversation ended, I advised him, "If you see someone who deserves a second chance, you give it to them, because you got one."

At that juncture, I still was unaware of the excessive force used against him by the transit police officer. It was later, when I interviewed Mr. Polyneice for this book, that he revealed this key information. If I had known it when I encountered him at the event, my advice would have been different. More specifically, I would have directed him to file a complaint against the officer. My hope was that in his capacity as prosecutor, if he saw someone whose case might deserve a deeper look, he take the time to see the full story.

Officers require training in the principles of procedural justice so they can perform their duties while respecting the citizens they are sworn to serve and protect. What we know about the benefits of such training is supported by data—as well as by common sense. Relations between police and communities, especially communities of color, must improve. The goal is to shift officers' perspective from "Everyone is a perp" to "I am responsible for the people in this community, and if someone makes a mistake I can hold them accountable, treat them with dignity and respect—and still offer them tools to prevent crime in the future."

* * *

These three major reforms—youth courts, violence reduction, and procedural justice in policing—present incredible possibilities for creating an exit ramp out of our criminal justice system. We can't continue to stand idly by while laws and school policies steer countless Black, Latinx, poor, and disabled young people into our prisons. We know that having any of these characteristics leads to receiving harsher discipline in school. In turn, being subjected to severe school discipline often leads to incarceration. Diversions and restorative justice practices are necessary to create a climate where children can learn, and where their youthful mistakes don't prevent them from living full lives.

Next, violence-reduction programs are essential to heal communities. We have to be in the business of returning people to their families and to society as contributing members. Using data to identify areas with high rates of violence and then targeting individuals in those neighborhoods for employment and social services is smart on crime.

And lastly, using procedural justice as a tenet of policing is a model geared toward improving trust in law enforcement and transforming officers into guardians of the community—true peace officers. Healing the community's relationship with the justice system begins here.

Chapter 7

REFORMED LEADERSHIP

I have to be honest. I can imagine a world where we are not required to live with unfairness. I believe we can change things for the better and improve people's lives. Treating people with respect can transform organizations and institutions. These skills are transferable. We first need to shift our perspectives to see how dignity and empathy can be centered in different environments. We need to ask tough questions and listen, even to uncomfortable truths. How do we conduct ourselves? What norms are we adhering to? How can we be better?

The courtroom is one of many possible settings where we can make an effort to improve how we engage the people we serve. It was where I wanted to make a contribution; I worked hard to continue improving how I treated individuals on both sides of the bench. If dignity, respect, and fairness are not fundamental standards in the courtroom environment, it can become like any other environment that is not true to its mission.

We first need to center around respect and dignity and then apply those principles everywhere. There was a time when we embraced the idea of treating each other with dignity wherever we were, whether church, school, or business. Today, disrespect is creeping into those and other settings, but it has been the norm within the justice system. People use disrespect as a form of entertainment across the internet, including social media, although it affects real lives. No longer do some people feel restrained when it comes to crossing what once were seen as boundaries imposed by social customs. It's time we look at every institution and every person we encounter and make a serious effort to apply the highest level of decency to everyone, everywhere.

I believe that the concepts and innovative approaches I've described in this book not only are relevant to the legal profession, but also can be applied to any business or organization. They can even be applied in one's personal life. Once we understand the power of restoring respect to our discourse, it will be contagious.

Procedural fairness, among other features, is about increasing the public's trust and restoring an institution's legitimacy. Businesses in a wide range of fields can certainly apply it. Once we infuse our organizations' cultures with this idea, we'll increase trust and improve relationships at all levels, inside and outside the business. For example, everyone knows how to deal with the best customer, but how do you deal with the worst customer? How do you deal with a person who may not be acting their best? How do you maintain standards in that situation?

The ideas in this book can help businesses improve their interactions with staff and customers. If an employee is struggling to meet performance goals, or if the relationship with a customer becomes challenging, the focus can shift away from punishment or reprimand. Having curiosity about what obstacles a person is facing, and taking the time to listen, can help a leader problem-solve in a way that not only restores the relationship but can motivate stronger outcomes. I believe the values of dignity and respect could be a company's secret weapon for increasing revenue and being honored in its community. Every institution in our society can play a part in accomplishing that.

As a leader, you have a role in shaping how respect and dignity play out in your community, whether you run the local store, an association, or a growing technology firm. No one in my life embodied these principles more than my mother, Ms. Elsa. She was an ally to the LGBTQ+ community before there was a name for it. She opened her heart and life to transgender women. A devout Catholic, my mother would say we were all God's children and we should be treated the same, and she meant everybody. Her adoptive daughter, Natalie Cordero, a transgender woman from Mom's beauty school days, was a fixture in my early life. My mother cooked for her, counseled her, and loved her.

Those leadership skills transferred to her business. My mom ensured that the beauty salon was a safe place for trans people who were transitioning. I remember a young Puerto Rican man, Ricardo, who came to the salon. Ricardo had gorgeous, long, jet-black hair. He arrived weekly for a roller set and to feel my mother's nurturing hands massage his scalp and to hear her endearing words fill his heart. As the months passed, we noticed that Ricardo began the process of transitioning to a woman by wearing more feminine clothing and applying eyeliner. No staring, snickering, or gossiping about Ricardo was permitted. The funny thing is that I never noticed anyone attempting to do so. I am confident that because my mother enveloped Ricardo with love, the other customers knew that gawking was unacceptable. Ms. Elsa knew how to guide the culture of her workplace, and she was gifted with a gentle, soft-spoken, yet powerful reprimand. She set the example and the standard for how people were to be treated, especially in the space she created—her salon. Years later, I ran into Ricardo after she had transitioned, although I did not know her new, female name. We embraced, she asked for my mom, and then she ran off for her train. She looked so happy. Her new life suited her.

Businesses and organizations of all sizes have immense power to set the tone in their communities. Leaders can create respectful, empathetic, and inclusive workplace communities through their day-to-day choices, including in hiring, guiding, and managing. Listening, giving people voice, and centering and supporting the marginalized can be part of the approach leaders take, even in advertising, sales, customer service, and public relations.

Businesses often underestimate the role they can play in impacting and defining culture, but they shouldn't. We can all be proactive in our practices. Do we train our employees to use words of respect? How do we treat patrons and vendors? Do we immediately respect the relationship and seek to deepen it with acts of dignity, or do we carelessly judge those we interact with by their race, appearance, or role? Below I've outlined five steps to applying my approach in businesses and organizations.

1. Prioritize Dignity and Respect

A leader must drive the idea of dignity and respect by defining policies that promote these values and writing them down.

This is not just a nice thing to do; it can set the course for both positive impact and positive growth in our organizations. Remember to make sure the statements are actionable.

In this step, we are shining a light on these concepts, and we should address them at all levels, including spelling out how we will execute them in our daily operations. Treat it as more than just a policy on paper; we need to be able to evaluate adherence to the process across all seniority levels, and in both internal and external interactions. As the chief judge of Newark Municipal Court, I noticed that departments were permitting employees to punch in and out according to their discretion. This often affected decisions to dock employees' pay. Reinforcing the policy on recording employees' time by issuing a memo ensured uniformity across the board.

Similarly, in the courtroom, we decided to post signs informing those who entered that the use of cell phones was prohibited. That way, people both saw the signs and later heard a verbal announcement about the phone policy. The dual messaging helped to set them up for success. The written signage also guaranteed that those who entered the courtroom late were informed of the prohibition.

To ensure that a message is filtering down and being enacted in practice, organizations must inform everyone in the organization that adherence is a priority. From the top executives to the secretaries to the janitors to the interns, everyone should be on the same page. A few ways to accomplish this is by instituting peer-to-peer reviews, addressing adherence in annual performance reviews, and including commentary on the messaging in reports to shareholders.

Most organizations can find it challenging to treat customers and others with dignity every day. How do you handle issues such as billing disputes? Do you have a script for handling a problematic client? Do you guard against bias, for example by resisting the assumption when a customer is a challenge that their behavior is typical for someone of their particular background?

Leaders should train employees to listen to, observe, and evaluate customer concerns with objectivity. People should always ask themselves, "Why do I have an automatic negative reaction to this provocation?" Training employees to be more formal in their approach is essential. Something as simple as taking an old-school approach in communication by addressing people as Mr. and Ms. can be a clear way to show respect. That way, employees can automatically check off certain boxes when engaging customers. Employees should learn from and comply with scripts that demonstrate they respect the customer.

Paying attention to how employees address a woman, a man, a member of the LGBTQ+ community, a person of color, a young person, or an old person—and the offhanded jokes they might make behind the scenes—should also be of vital concern. A lack of respect for individuals may be a sign of deep-seated bigotry that needs to be addressed.

This approach can call others to leadership. A couple of years ago, I accepted an invitation to a birthday party in California. When I phoned my friend to receive the details, the birthday girl informed me that she and her guests would spend her birthday in Pelican Bay State Prison working with the participants in her program, which teaches inmates how to be entrepreneurs. *Absolutely not*, I thought as this crazy friend spoke enthusiastically. No way, no how, were you getting me to enter a prison voluntarily. Judges have to be the most unwelcome visitors in prison. Why would I subject myself to that?

When I mentioned the plan to my husband, Paul, he said, "You have to go if you want to be able to speak about reform in the entire justice system."

Really? Your wife should go to a male prison. I was terrified simply thinking of the disdain I would be met with. The California Department of Corrections sent the most violent inmates to Pelican Bay, the state's only supermax prison. This included men who had infractions at other prisons.

I decided to go, hoping to make a contribution to the people I would meet. When it was my turn to stand in front of the group assembled in the gym, the speaker introduced me as a judge. I felt the looks of surprise, shock, condemnation, even contempt. I decided to use my only weapon: treat them with dignity and respect. When I stepped forward to speak, I did what I always do—I related an impactful story. It was a story that had been shared with me about bull elephants in South Africa. (I learned later that it came from Gus van Dyk's work on juvenile delinquency in young male elephants.)[1] I usually tell my altered version of the story to men appearing in my court who are forty to fifty years old. It speaks to their lives.

As we know, elephants typically are docile by nature. They are vegetarians, and they only attack when provoked. The male, the strong alpha, is massive, weighing upwards of eleven thousand pounds. There was a reservation in South Africa that was overpopulated with elephants. To relieve the congestion, the park-keepers came up with a plan to transport some of the elephants to another South African preserve. To accomplish this, they built harnesses to airlift the elephants.

They successfully airlifted and transported the baby elephants and then the female adult elephants. When it came time to transport the male adult elephants, they ran into a tremendous problem: the harness straps weren't strong enough to hold them. Then someone came up with a brilliant idea. The park-keepers could resolve the issue by leaving all the adult male elephants at the original reservation and transporting all the baby elephants and female adult elephants to the other one.

After the transferred elephants arrived at their new home, the park-keepers there realized they had a problem: the endangered rhinos were being killed at an alarming rate. The park-keepers believed that poachers were coming onto the grounds at night, hunting and killing the rhinos. They decided to put up cameras so they could catch the culprits in the act.

Now, they were curious about why poachers would leave the incredibly valuable rhino horns behind. Two pounds of a rhino's horn is worth about $65,000 on the black market. Much to their surprise, the footage revealed that young male elephants were wandering around the park at night in packs, attacking and killing the rhinos. The young male elephants gored and stomped the rhinos, absolutely unprovoked. They were acting outside their nature.

The park-keepers decided to send the baby male elephants back to the original preserve, where they would reside with the adult male elephants. When the young male elephants were returned, the adult males got them in order. They shoved and pushed them into line. They disciplined them and showed them how to behave. By being reunited with adult males, the baby male elephants were exposed to behavior they could model.

I told the prisoners that is precisely what has happened in our communities as a result of the war on drugs. Men have been removed from our communities in the act of mass incarceration. They swell jails and prisons, leaving young men without grown-male behavior to model. Our young men are behaving outside their nature. I told the group,

> Instead of sitting in here feeling sorry for yourself, you have a responsibility to tell those young men the truth. These young guys revere you, and they are lining up on the outside to come in here. They are trying to get in here to be with you to prove a point. What you need to do is to tell them the truth about this horrible experience. Tell them about not being able to have your liberty and freedom—not being able to eat your steak with a knife, not being able to brush your teeth or bathe when you want. Call your sons, your nephews, your godsons, your little brothers, and tell them to keep themselves out of here. You have these eighteen-year-old boys in the streets running entire gangs. I don't understand how any self-respecting adult could be taking orders from a child—much less let them raise your sons and your nephews and do nothing about it.

The prisoners gave me a standing ovation. The following day, I returned for more training. Many of them approached me and introduced themselves, and I shook their hands. I listened closely to them without interrupting. One younger guy patiently waited. He looked no more than thirty, and he wore a tattoo between his hazel-brown eyes that stood out against his bisque-colored skin. He extended his hand and said, "Judge, I just wanted to thank you for sharing that story. It really touched me." He placed his hand over his heart and continued,

> I went back on the yard and told everybody about the elephant story. I even called home and told the story. Then

I called my homie on the outside, and he started talking to me about these street beefs and how he couldn't wait till I got home to rough people up and set them straight. I stopped him and said, "You think I've wasted all these years in here to come out and do the same thing that got me in here?" I told *him* the story of the elephants. I told him we've got to change. We've got to start mentoring these young people. We got to be role models to these young homies.

In total disbelief, I asked, "That's what you told him?"

He nodded proudly. He told me how his homies were planning a cookout the following Saturday to raise some money to buy sports equipment for the young people in the community.

I looked at him, and I said, "You understand that's how much power you have here, right? You have this power to influence minds. What are you going to use this for? For a criminal enterprise, or to save your community and stop seeing these young guys, like you, come into this place?"

Numerous men continued to approach me. A young Cambodian man told me, "Your story really touched me." He rolled up his sleeve, revealing an elaborate tattoo of an elephant. "The elephant is my spirit animal."

He explained how there was an absence of adult elephants in his community as well. The men left, never to return. I listened intently as he talked about feeling unloved as a young person. When he finished, I told him, "I've been observing you as you work the room. You are a peer mentor in this program. Everyone you interact with bursts into a smile or laughter. You could change their whole disposition for the better.

Who better to give love than someone who was deprived of it? Some of us receive love by pouring it into others."

It's immensely powerful to witness people tapping into that thing they're supposed to do. And I don't mean the easy thing that does not require effort. I mean the thing that stretches them beyond their self-imposed limitations.

Treating people with dignity and respect is about people-centered leadership. I shared a story with the inmates that spoke directly to them. I entered the prison as a person in authority who did not come into the environment to condemn them further. Instead, I came to encourage them to take action that would have a positive impact on the communities they had harmed. My leadership role was to inspire the men to become better leaders. As incarcerated gang members, they wielded enormous power over the young people who remained in their neighborhoods. While they were experiencing one of the worst circumstances a human being could endure, I spoke to them respectfully and gave them a voice. And in that voice, they began to examine how to redirect their leadership skills. The last person they wanted to see in prison was a judge. Their final impression of fairness most likely had been delivered by a judge. Hopefully, their experience with me that day improved it.

Leadership can prioritize the dignity of everyone in the room, creating a foundation for people to feel inspired to do more and do better. The best leaders don't have to order people to perform or threaten them with punishment. They inspire and motivate to get the best out of a group—even a roomful of inmates. If I could overcome hurdles in that prison, any leader can use dignity to spark a better work culture and motivate better performance among their staff.

2. See Beyond the Surface

A leader must care enough to take time to get to the bottom of issues that arise. When it comes to problematic staff or clients, a business leader may be tempted to use aggressive tactics, including complaints, demands for change, formal discipline, threats of firing, or the silent treatment. Stepping back and empathizing with someone whose behavior is irritating or counterproductive may require humility—but taking that extra step of going deeper, listening harder, taking a breath, and being curious about extenuating factors can be essential in problem-solving. If a leader's only method of control is aggression, for transgressions big or small, it can wear away the trust between the leader and the group they are meant to serve.

Even before I became a judge, I found that reaching a greater understanding of issues was a vital leadership skill. After doing a stint in the New Jersey governor's office as assistant counsel of the Authorities Unit, I decided to take on the job of Camden City School District's compliance officer. Many wondered why I would do it. "Everyone knows that place is full of corruption, and they don't take kindly to outsiders" was the message I heard. Well, there's a rap song called "Never Scared." I often embody this lyric, even when I am scared, and I forge forward despite those fears. How could I turn my back on children who were within my reach to help? Yes, it would be a challenge, but I went there with one aim in mind—to ensure that young people were receiving the resources they needed to be able to learn and to build lives for themselves.

The governor's office provided the city of Camden $75 million for economic development. The city was required to make certain concessions to obtain the money, namely giving the governor veto power over items on the school board's minutes and accepting three governor appointees as voting members to the school board. The governor could essentially undo any actions taken by the school board. I was sent in to monitor the board's activities and make reports. I was called a snitch, yelled at, and even threatened by community members. But I knew what I was getting myself into, or so I thought.

One of my responsibilities was to preapprove specific requests for expenditures from the schools in the district. One day, the assistant superintendent entered my office, dropped papers on my desk, and said, "Didn't you tell them not to have so many paid meetings? You deal with them and all these invoices."

Two elementary schools had submitted payment vouchers for compensation for student leadership committee meetings. Student leadership committees, or teams as they are also known, were composed of parents, school staff, and administrators who created student success policies. Schools submitted budgets for the meetings that ranged from $2,000 to $24,000 per year. For the sake of uniformity and to reduce spending, I advised each school that it would be permitted to have only one paid meeting per month. All other meetings would have to be voluntary.

I was quite surprised that these two schools had each submitted about eight payment vouchers for three months. I contacted one of the schools and told them I would not approve the vouchers. They resubmitted the vouchers by whiting out the sign-in sheets and including new dates. I decided to take a closer look at the meeting documents.

I'd had initial concerns about these two schools because their extremely high test scores were questionable. Their third graders' test results indicated they were 100 percent and 98 percent proficient, respectively, in reading comprehension and math. This is a district plagued by generational poverty, homelessness, and abysmal health outcomes. Not to mention that Camden was listed the most dangerous city in America for a number of years. Some of the students were bused in from surrounding homeless shelters.

My investigation found that none of the meetings had taken place. School staff were forging documents in an attempt to steal school funds. When I sought to continue my investigations, I was met by an attempt to shut me down. What I didn't understand at the time was that bonuses were paid out as a result of the high test results from those two schools. With the assistance of the school board president, I conducted a full investigation. I needed to determine why people who had been employed with the school district for so long would jeopardize themselves and their pensions for such insignificant amounts of money.

The assistant superintendent and I decided that we would simultaneously confront the employees whose signatures appeared on the documents. When I arrived at one of the schools, I could feel the tension in the air. An employee directed me to the library, where the teachers and teacher's aides were seated around the table. They were visibly frightened. I began by showing them the signatures on sign-in pages with the original dates and then the altered dates. I explained that what had happened was a violation of district policies and the law. I explained that I already knew that no meetings had taken place, so there was no point in denying it. I said I needed to know what happened. And they needed to come clean.

I told them that if they were afraid to share information in the group setting, they could speak to me individually. I ensured that they understood the consequences of what would happen, which included turning the matter over to the police department. Although I was representing the school district, I told them I would help them if they told me what they knew. I began to probe them with questions: "Who told you to sign?" "When did you sign?" "Why did you sign?" "Why would you risk your jobs?" "What other things have you been told to do?"

Like a falling house of dominoes, one by one they began to explain that the school principal had called them to his office. He had assigned them to the student leadership committees and instructed them to sign their names on the sign-in sheets. They were all afraid to refuse the principal or his minions. This principal was so closely connected to the district leadership that it almost derailed my investigation. They had seen the repercussions for failing to comply with his demands.

At the other school, however, the assistant superintendent had no luck with the employees. No one cooperated with the investigation. They all remained loyal to the principal. I believe that the assistant superintendent's curt and condescending approach failed to convince school staff to defect. They remained loyal to the principal even when the principal retired early in an attempt to save their pension and leave the employees holding the bag. The employees at that school either were fired, lost tenure, or were indicted and convicted.

At the school I was investigating, I treated the employees with dignity and respect, even though they were in trouble. I afforded them opportunities to have a voice, either in the group or separately. I showed them that I cared about the situation and believed them. Using my authority, I offered them cover if they cooperated. They would be held accountable, but their cooperation would mitigate the severity of their punishment.

It was important that I understood their circumstances and that they knew I understood. Tyrannical principals had been allowed to intimidate and coerce staff without recourse. Some employees observed how I treated their coworkers during my investigations and decided to cooperate after years of being strong-armed into remaining silent about corruption. They had been waiting to be heard and freed from the oppressive clutches of the principals and their underlings.

Seeing beneath the surface in this matter led to the uncovering of myriad schemes against the school district by two principals, including the theft of field trip money from parents and teachers, who had paid for field trips that were in fact covered by the school district. When the testing of fourth graders, who had tested off the charts as third graders, was monitored, scores plummeted from the preceding year.

Even more important than the findings, however, through my investigation I came to understand the environment that had allowed corruption to flourish. After the Campbell Soup Company closed its operations in Camden, the school district became the only major employer in the city. Being fired from the school district would lead to longtime, irreparable hardship. The school principals were keenly aware of this fact, and two of them used it to pressure and punish subordinates. Those fiefdoms needed to be dismantled. The focus needed to be centered on weeding out the damaging forces to protect the children.

We must develop a cultural understanding of the people we interact with, whether they are customers, clients, or employees. Doing so will assist us in understanding what motivates them. It will also provide us with a clearer understanding of the circumstances under which they act. What are their trigger points? What motivates them to change and to accept change?

As we stand in our professional roles, it isn't easy to conceptualize that caring about people will help us meet our goals. Many of us don't even know how to express empathy in the workplace. By asking probing questions, you can express care and develop a deeper understanding of people and their circumstances. Questions should be intended to elicit relevant answers that give you a greater appreciation of the individuals you're interacting with.

As we make inquiries, we should also consider practicing the art of shutting up—to listen intently without speaking. To listen intently involves restraint. And for people in positions of authority, that may be a challenge. People frequently come to us with problems that require solving. Often, we react without taking time to understand exactly what situation needs to be addressed, leaving the speaker feeling ignored and insignificant. The art of shutting up allows us to focus on the person and their concerns.

In the Camden school district, when I listened to the subordinates, I could hear the fear in their voices. I heard them say they felt powerless against the two principals, who could do no wrong in the eyes of the superintendent because of their schools' high test scores, even though the scores were questionable. My investigations proved the employees' worries to be true. In addition to repercussions from their bosses, they would have faced a negative backlash from a faction in the community vested in maintaining the culture of corruption. I speak from experience as someone who had a chair kicked in her direction when the school board fired an employee due to my findings. The employees needed to be held accountable because their actions harmed children. However, they, too, were victims of the school district's culture. Firing them would have been a punishment too severe. They had continued to serve the children despite the wrongdoing of the leadership. Holding people accountable can help rebuild trust destroyed by years of corruption.

Years later, as a judge, I painfully watched another judge who couldn't practice the art of shutting up. I observed this judge for a day, hoping to get some pointers; instead, I was sorely disappointed. The judge was paternalistic and arrogant. Defendants came to court with various low-level offenses and visible issues. The judge would wave their arms around, and sometimes the gavel, as if they were some kind of wizard. They created rehabilitation plans for defendants. The problem was they didn't spend any time asking the defendants probing questions to determine their true needs. They refused to rely on the expertise of the clinicians who had years of experience dealing with the issues. If the defendants did not participate in the remedies they were assigned, why would they care about the outcome? You see this behavior in organizations where people are not consulted about their needs. They merely go through the motions.

3. Meet People Where They Are

A leader must be adept at listening to others and sensing what they do and don't understand. This applies in every relationship within an organization. Do we know the mindsets of our employees and vendors? Do we respect customers and the role we play in their busy, complicated lives? Or do we judge those we interact with by their appearance or even race? Do we create situations where we can truly hear others—and they can hear us?

To encourage others to assimilate new ideas and new strategies, you have to earn their trust. Otherwise, you will be unable to convince them to do anything. Dictating is not an answer. We must be in a position to hear people, and then help them into a position where they can hear us. This principle required me to meet the many players who entered my courtroom where they were.

We often learn about leadership, dignity, and respect through our dealings with local businesses and institutions. However, we may give little thought to how powerful this community-level interaction can be. One reason might be that our society is less formal than it once was, resulting in a casual and almost careless attitude toward others. We can sometimes see this callousness in our daily interactions, even before we get to institutions like courts.

When we started Newark Community Solutions, our community court program, one of the program's staunch opponents was a public defender. She held firm to her belief that her job was to zealously advocate for her clients' release, without requiring anything else. Offering services to her clients as a condition of the release wasn't in the equation. She advised her clients not to participate in the program.

After a conflict with her boss, the public defender was sent to my court on a thirty-day rotation as a form of punishment. The boss knew that she and I did not see eye to eye and anticipated that we would become embroiled in conflict due to her objection to admitting defendants to the program. The supervisor also hoped the conflict might eventually get the employee terminated. I decided that I would accept her position and re-schedule potential defendants who may have wanted to partic-ipate in the program to a date after her assignment in my court ended.

During the following weeks, while not recommending the program to any of her current clients, this public defender ob-served previously admitted people coming to court and receiv-ing positive feedback as they read their essays. I would ask her what she thought about certain essays. I would also ask her to help with our work—for example, I'd say, "Madam public de-fender, I need you to go outside and talk to the defendant and make sure their mind is right before they come back in here with their foolishness."

I noticed that she began to participate in the clapping. She proudly stood next to her clients who successfully completed the program. She even began to praise clients who were in the program. Something in the atmosphere of the courtroom started to slip into her. Before long, she was recommending that her clients participate in the program. A miracle. As her last week in my court approached, she said, "I'm actually go-ing to miss it here. It's nice to see the people coming back and doing well."

Initially, she had rejected the program. Meeting her where she was meant I needed to take my ego out of the situation and accept her position. I needed her to see the value of the program, and that required relationship building. If we can comprehend what's said, then we allow ourselves to hear it.

Poet Johann Wolfgang von Goethe said, "Our understand-ing of people is limited by what we can take in." I didn't need to enlist this public defender in the revolution immediately. I understood that her training required her to advocate for her clients' release without any conditions. If I wanted her to become a part of this new ideology, I could show her better than I could tell her. This had to be done one day at a time, in small, incremental steps. She began to come around. When she left the community court, she started referring cases to us from other courtrooms.

We must invest time in a person—and in relationship building—to see that person's circumstances and point of view. It is critical to understand that we all grow in stages. Change is often slow and gradual, pushed along by consistent behavior or reinforcement. Usually, we must modify our initial expectations to get people where we want them to be.

4. Solve Problems Innovatively

Why don't we engage in creative problem-solving? Because it is easier to follow convention. It is easier to swim with the current, even when the current dumps you into a toxic cesspool. By following a traditional script, we don't learn anything new. Our ability to attack a problem from a different angle is also impeded.

Ask yourself, "How much am I doing by rote? Could I do this with my eyes closed?" If so, interrupt your process. Break your pattern so that you can generate better outcomes when attempting to resolve problems as a leader. You must be willing to look into the shadows to see what is obscured. As an innovator in the courtroom, using dignity, respect, and fairness as my guide, I did that instinctively while speaking to defendants and asking them questions about themselves. I'm naturally curious about people. It's intuitive for me to ask them questions. I find people fascinating.

Being innovative requires uncovering new ways to solve challenges. Innovation often calls for doing the obvious in an environment devoted to processes that don't work. Perhaps counterintuitively, innovation is sometimes doing what should have been apparent.

In their book *Good Courts: The Case for Problem-Solving Justice*, Greg Berman and John Feinblatt lay out the best practices they've observed in specialized courts across the country:[2]

- **Reexamine your goals.** When faced with a challenging situation, reimagine your outcomes. What does success look like if you shift your focus toward better outcomes for all parties?

- **Make the most of authority.** Tap into your position of authority to increase compliance. While people in authority don't always have to use their most punitive tool to ensure compliance, they should be aware of incentives they can offer to motivate people.

- **Put problems in context.** Take the time to consider all factors in a given situation, and push yourself toward a deeper understanding of any underlying issues. Don't make the problem something it is not because of an emotional trigger.

- **Form creative partnerships.** Add new voices to the conversation in order to source possible new solutions. Partner with those who may be closer to the situation. Look for people with more expertise who can help you dissect and attack the problem.

- **Rethink traditional roles.** Consider whether the traditional managerial roles of enforcing hierarchy, applying rules, and threatening punishment can at times be limiting. Leaders across seniority levels and job functions must undertake the roles of nurturer, teacher, counselor, and problem-solver. Different problems need different approaches. Leaders should broaden their range of skills by reconsidering the conventions of their role and status.

It can be difficult to find ways to apply these principles in every situation, but the results can be rewarding. I recall one case in particular that required creative problem-solving, when Anthony Aziz entered my courtroom. Looking up from reviewing his file, I saw a defiant smirk that seemed permanently installed on his young face. With his head tilted to the side and his frame swimming in his oversized shirt, he just looked silly. "Lord, give me strength," I couldn't help but murmur.

This young man was going to try my patience. He had a marijuana possession charge and refused to show up on time for his court-ordered mandates. It was as if he was daring me to send him to the county jail. Once there, he would earn his stripes. Getting sent to jail was often a rite of passage that earned a young person street cred and respect from their friends. I wouldn't give it to him.

Months earlier, I had discontinued the use of the essay topic "Where Do I See Myself When I Turn Twenty-Five Years Old?" Inevitably, young men wrote that they didn't expect to see twenty-one, much less twenty-five. The despair and fatalism that poured out of these defendants was too much for me to bear. But I could tell that even a different essay prompt wouldn't get Mr. Aziz where he needed to be. Assigning an essay wasn't going to work with him, and jail was not an option. How would I reach him?

I decided to talk to him about his potential. When I mentioned college, he interrupted with a loud laugh, and his whole body swayed. "College? Come on, Judge. Don't no Black men from Newark go to college." He looked at me as if I had just landed from another planet.

"What?! Newark is full of Black men who went to college. And I went to college with a bunch of them," I countered.

Contrite, he responded, "I ain't never seen any."

And there was the problem. He couldn't become that which he had never seen.

I called a court recess, went into my chambers, and contacted Keith Hamilton, one of those Black men from Newark who'd gone to college with me. He was working next door in city hall as a legislative aide for then councilman (and future mayor) Ras Baraka. I explained what had transpired and told him that I needed him to take Mr. Aziz into his office as an intern. He needed to be surrounded by educated Black men. He needed to see them, hear them, speak to them, and be immersed in their way of thinking.

I returned to court and advised the young man of the arrangement. He would work with Mr. Hamilton, whose office would provide me with a report. Mr. Aziz couldn't say it in court, but once the internship was offered, it was clear that he longed for mentorship. During the assignment, he learned about civics, heard about people's concerns in community meetings, and passed along to city staff constituents' reports about potholes and downed trees so the issues could be addressed. He had an opportunity to observe and emulate streetwise college-educated men and not just gangsters. He completed the program and never returned to court. Throughout the years I enlisted many community folks to serve as mentors, such as attorney

Anton Lendor, boxing coach Derrick Graham, and Gary Paul Wright of the African American Office of Gay Concerns, to name a few. I assigned many young men mentors through these internships.

Instead of creating a plan for Mr. Aziz within the typical confines of the judicial system, I had innovated using the principles stated above. I reexamined the initial goal of punishment to force compliance. To shift his behavior, I decided it was more important to meet his needs. I used my judicial authority to direct his actions and engage others in his change process. I reframed the problem. Yes, he was smoking marijuana, which was illegal at the time, and he was headed down the wrong path. However, the real problem was that he didn't think he had any other options for his life. Our justice system has to correctly diagnose the problem to cure the condition that brings someone to the courtroom. We cannot solely focus on and punish people for the symptoms. Resolve the real issue and the symptoms disappear.

I also formed a creative partnership with the legislative branch, an action that is often frowned upon. Still, in this case it allowed city officials to directly help a citizen who was part of a problem that constituents complain about daily: crime. Their office was as close to the problem as you could get. I knew Newark men who had escaped the same traps that this young man was walking into. They went on to obtain their education and came back to serve their community. Using an innovative approach to problem-solving required the court and the staff to change their roles to assist Mr. Aziz. My role as the person who metes out punishment for poor behavior had to be substituted with the role of troubleshooter. I decided to step aside from the traditional role to engage others to get this defendant where he needed to be. Punishment for defiance and noncompliance was imminent. However, that wasn't what he needed.

There are clear parallels here for managers at all levels and in all types of organizations across the country. You will have colleagues, employees, clients, and customers who seem difficult, who don't perform well, who won't behave the way you need them to. You can see them as problematic individuals who need to be dealt with, punished, threatened, or cut off. Or you can see them as people who are struggling, who may need support—who may not even know how to ask for help. The tools I've suggested allow you to problem-solve in a creative, generative way, which can produce lasting benefits for all parties. Engendering obedience and smooth operations is one set of goals—but many goals can best be met through motivating people and building relationships, allowing everyone to meet their potential.

5. Don't Ignore Common Sense

When I became a judge and assessed my new role, I knew something for certain. I had to do what was within my authority and the law, but I also had to do the best I could for those who came before me in courtroom 222.

Doing what's in the best interest of the child is a legal doctrine used during child custody battles. A judge needs to determine the rights of the child and analyze and balance those rights alongside the needs of the adults involved in the case. The hope is that this balancing method will include a commonsense approach, an act of wisdom. Samuel Taylor Coleridge, the English poet, expounded, "Common sense in an uncommon degree is what the world calls wisdom."

In our society, in businesses, and in other organizations, we often believe that only the most complex strategy, intricate algorithm, or convoluted policy will resolve challenges. But sometimes those tactics are not aligned with the best outcome. By focusing on what makes sense, what's in front of us, we can resolve problems and get to the bottom of issues. We should focus on more than attacking the superficial concern. We should always be interested in the underlying matter. For example, is it best to impose a fine on someone who is already incapable of paying court fees? Does it make sense to automatically arrest someone on a minor offense simply because you can? Might it be best to warn a citizen they're in danger of breaking a law that could have serious consequences, rather than sitting back and watching it unfold?

Whether you are in a position of authority or not, we all have a responsibility to do what's best for one another, even if that is unconventional and unpopular. In the criminal justice system, commission of an offense is usually a symptom of an underlying condition, and a commonsense approach is to consider what that condition might be.

In court, I often found that the best decision was the practical one. On a busy summer afternoon, a woman entered the courtroom with a little boy around seven or eight. I assumed they were there to see a person who was in police custody. This child would now see someone he cared about come out in handcuffs. The day was going to be even longer than I had expected. I noticed that the court officer spent a long time speaking to the woman. The young boy sat there pouting his lips, his little arms defiantly crossed and his little head balancing a bushel of hair in a neat Afro. He was the cutest thing. The officer approached the bench to tell me that the mom was having trouble with her eight-year-old son and wanted me to talk to him. The exhausted judge in me thought, *With all this work I have to do here? I'm not going to talk to another person.* However, the practical judge in me thought, *My pleasure.*

I arched my eyebrow and said sternly from the bench, "Young man, uncross your arms in my courtroom. It makes me think you have an attitude about something." Shocked, he immediately dropped them to his side.

I called him up with his mom, and he looked down bashfully. He ran his hands across the table as his mother outlined his behavior. "Judge, he got suspended from school and didn't tell me," she began. "The next day, he got dressed and went to school anyway. When they asked him why he came back to school, he told them, 'My mom said she is not taking off from work, so y'all have to give me an in-school suspension.'"

Students subjected to an in-school suspension cannot go to regular classes but must report to a room where they are monitored by a teacher or dean. A 2018 study showed that Black students in K–12 were suspended or expelled at a rate 3.2 times higher than their white counterparts. As adults, these individuals showed higher rates of being involved in crime, being victims of crime, and incarceration.[3]

He's brilliant, I thought, impressed by the boy's ability to reason and spin a yarn.

After a couple of days of in-school suspension, the principal demanded to see his mom. She picked up the narrative. "The principal brought in the police and asked [my son] to take them to our home. They were looking for me. This boy took them way across town to our old house. Then he told the police that I wasn't home."

You could hear muffled chuckles in the courtroom. I shook my head and looked at him without smiling. This was incredible.

Exasperated, the mom said, "The police finally figured out where we lived and brought him to our house. When they got to our house, he told the police, 'No, I play there; I don't live there.'"

This child's storytelling talent could be dangerous if not appropriately channeled. I talked to him about the consequences of his actions. I asked him about his favorite subject in school. He told me it was math. I assigned him an essay and gave him a date to come back to read it.

Two weeks later, the boy returned to court with his mom to read his essay. He wore a white tank top and walked confidently. He showed me that he had filled out the entire sheet of paper. His essay was titled "Why I Love Math," but when he began to read, he only whispered. He had a hard time getting started. When his mother stood next to him, his whole demeanor turned sour. I said, "Mom, sit down. You're making him nervous." She returned to her seat.

Then the men in the courtroom, the police officers, and the public defender decided to gather around him and encourage him. He immediately stood up straighter. He felt supported. It was a great essay, and he earned a round of applause.

But his mother didn't clap; she was agitated. She yelled, "He's been getting in trouble since he left here! He set off firecrackers in the house! He is playing with fire!"

This is getting serious, I thought. He was spinning a show for us, too, making the room think he was complying and behaving himself, when he wasn't. He was a child, and we needed to figure it out. I told him that an arson charge would get him sent directly to the youth house. I told his mom to bring him to court the next day so he could work with us. Maybe pouring some love into him would help.

To serve this family's best interest required that I engage the boy as if he had a court date, even though I had no jurisdiction over him. His mom was at her wit's end. She had brought him that first day because someone had told her the judge down at the courthouse helps young people. It only makes sense that the court would act preemptively in this young man's life. It could have been easy to send them away, in light of the court's busy calendar. But common sense meant taking a deeper look to see what was going on.

The child's behavior was triggered by anger toward his mom. We were able to offer them assistance through the Newark Community Solutions clinic of social workers. He was a brilliant young man whom I didn't want to see in ten years. The most practical and obvious strategy was to engage him now. A lot of care and encouragement, and a little intimidation, was the formula I had at my disposal. And the men in the courtroom were able to mentor and advise.

The concept of doing what's best, using common sense, also has relevance for running a business. Management consultants are paid to help organizations align with their mission statements. This might mean developing a culture where you are always trying to do what is best for the customer and employee. During the COVID-19 pandemic, the government asked millions of people to stay home. It was important to keep telephone and internet service going. Telecommunications companies across the country didn't worry about collecting payments that were owed to them. Instead, maintaining services just made sense for the public and society as a whole. Certainly, if you ask everyone to stay home, you can make sure they are not cut off from the world.

If companies were always harsh about the bottom line, they'd lose trust with their customers. The companies who want to model good citizenship do what's right and pool resources to help the community—and this is, in fact, good business, since it shows a company's commitment to people's needs in times of crisis. The corporations that instead focus only on profits and take advantage of people's hardships are not going to be remembered well when the crisis is over. This is just common sense.

The Walt Disney Company has a basic policy regarding how it treats customers at its theme parks: Make the guest happy. Notice two things here: First, the ingenious use of the word "guest"—not patron or customer. This is someone who's been invited into Disney's environment. Second, notice the simplicity of the policy—make them happy. Those who work at Disneyland have an obvious charge to do whatever they can to create this result. If they see that a child has dropped their ice cream cone on the pavement, employees have the authority, the responsibility, to replace that ice cream cone for free. If short-term profits were the only motivation, it wouldn't make sense to lose money in that situation—but a child's memories will last a lifetime. Using common sense about human relationships can, in the long run, build a loyal customer base.

So how does this concept relate to other kinds of businesses and organizations? First, most leaders do not empower their people with such a noble vision. They should. Second, unfortunately, for many employees, the idea of being the best at their vocation is a foreign concept. Many are just trying to get by, to avoid trouble with the boss, to not ruffle feathers with col-leagues. Instead, we should all be empowered to use common sense, and if the official rules aren't useful, we should take steps to make things better. Imagine if we established aligning with a commonsense approach as an objective in our organizations and homes. We'd have fewer people in court and fewer mis-understandings that could blossom into legal battles and, even worse, confrontations.

If you're running a retail business, are you inclined to as-sume that the young Black kid is shoplifting and follow them around? Could the young man dressed in a hoodie and jeans be a promising young student and not a threat? Could he be a young entrepreneur? Could the young lady who enters the bank wanting to open a business account be an ambitious retailer rather than suspicious? Thinking the best of others is a com-monsense approach because it allows us to be problem-solvers and not problem-finders.

***

The desire and need to improve service and working envi-ronments exists across industries. Embracing these principles requires only a commitment from leadership to enact change. Leaders cannot blame the failings of their organizations solely on troublesome employees—"If they only fell in line, every-thing would go according to plan." Rather, leaders must ac-knowledge their role in the outcomes they are witnessing.

I once spoke about leadership skills at a large employee meeting for a company that sells financial products. Applying my approach to their industry felt very natural. In a business where dealing with customers' money makes you money, and where you have a fiduciary relationship, the work requires the building of trust. Often people who are selling us things assume that their expertise is all we need to feel comfortable in the relationship. But to build trust with potential clients, you need to treat them with dignity and respect in every transaction. You can't talk down to a client, or dismiss their concerns out of hand. Overwhelming a client with industry jargon to show off your superior knowledge or bragging about how much better you are than the competitors won't work in establishing a new relationship. Trust needs to be built on common ground. You have to meet the client where they are. You should ensure that they feel respected, and that they understand what you are presenting, especially when your business is complex and nonintuitive. They need to feel good about choosing your company.

Financial professionals, for example, must have the humility and patience to listen closely so they can get to the heart of what their clients desire. People often come to them with limited knowledge about the products they're selling. Meeting people where they are in this case means making sure they understand the language. If the client trusts the advisor, they are more likely to believe that what's being offered is in their best interest. They need to know that you are not putting them at an outsized risk. You may even have an opportunity to engage in creative problem-solving when trying to help a client meet their financial goals. And again, always use common sense: "Do they need term or whole life insurance right now?"

My mother intuitively knew the importance of these skills in operating her small business, and I learned to apply them in the courtroom. They can improve the delivery of service in all sorts of industries—medical, educational, and retail—and can be scaled up for organizations of any size. Whether a business is fostering relationships with customers or a nonprofit is doing community outreach, trust has to be foregrounded. The key is to bring respect and empathy to every situation. Humility and the ability to listen are essential. Anyone can use the principles of respect to transform their workplace. Any workplace can make an impact on its community. Respect can flow out to stretch across neighborhoods and the nation. When you see the power of dignity affecting the life of just one vulnerable person, you won't want to keep the message to yourself. These lessons are for all communities, all enterprises—for everyone. They restore people's dignity, which is a universal need.

The criminal justice system often defaults to the harshest penalties for low-level offenders. Schools embrace polices that impose disproportionate discipline. Companies rely on hiring practices that fail to value diversity and inclusion. Broken-windows tactics in policing demonize Black, mentally ill, poor, and other marginalized people, pushing them away from mainstream society, denying them the opportunity to live ordinary, perhaps even exceptional lives. As their frustration deepens, the farther they stray. Worse, the individuals most severely affected by such policies don't have a voice in the policy decisions. Why must we treat a large section of the population as if they are beyond redemption? What chance do we give them to live full lives?

The corrosive nature of the justice system's relationship with the people it serves helped motivate my determination to make an impact. The culture shift will take time, maybe years. In the face of what appears immovable, I affirm my commitment by reminding myself *I'm built for this. Stay focused on the goal, no matter what's going on.* I once heard that respect is a long lesson in self-control. Humans must make a lifelong commitment to the practice of self-control, because without it we cannot maintain the dignity of others. In the absence of dignity and respect there is no justice.

This mindset is my journey to justice. These life-affirming lessons of dignity, respect, and fairness need to be incorporated and reimagined in how we interact.

A LETTER TO MY SON

My dearest Hendrick,

As the judge who assigns reflective essays, I thought it was befitting to assign myself one. Essays with the title "A Letter to My Son/Daughter" are among the most powerful I've heard defendants read in court. I've seen them transform many lives. And so I'm writing to tell you what I've come to know, and why I believe my work serving the public is so important. I want to share my reflections on how I hope I've contributed to reforming my community. I hope to pass on to you the same community-honoring values that your grandparents gave to me, and I hope these life lessons will help you and anyone who may come across this work.

First, as the mother of an African American, Latino, and Haitian little boy, I hope that my life's work creates a safe and just space where you can grow and prosper. My daily prayer is that you flourish and realize the great potential I already see in you. You are an incredible, talented, and brilliant human, and you deserve a clear path toward a fulfilling life. You see, if the country and the world are safe places in which you can flourish, then they are most likely also safe for all little Black and Brown boys and girls—and for *all* children.

These are the values instilled in me by your grandparents: everyone should feel respected, should believe they matter, and should be treated with dignity and fairness. Whenever I worry whether my efforts to instill the same values into the criminal justice system have been in vain, I receive evidence of the impact those efforts have made. "My judge does everything that you just talked about," a court clerk once said to me. She had walked up to me in the hallway after one of my presentations on procedural justice. I was in Denver, Colorado, for the third time, presenting to a group of judges and their staff. The court clerk was determined to let me know that unlike some of the other judges, the one she worked for already treated people with dignity and respect. When I asked her who this spectacular judge might be, I realized I knew the judge she was talking about.

During lunch, I told the judge what her clerk had said, and she responded, "That's because of you. I attended a three-day seminar on procedural justice you conducted in San Diego, and I came back to my courtroom and changed everything I did. Now I love my job. I'm not interested in moving up. I want to be right where I can make a difference in people's lives."

Another time, I was in Scotland when a judge approached me and said that we had a friend in common. I was certain that she was wrong as I didn't know anyone in Scotland. She said, "A judge from Trinidad called me and told me you would be in Scotland and to make sure that I got to hear you speak because you revolutionized the way she did her job."

Moments like these gratify me. And not just because I affected a judge, but because that judge's leadership inspired her staff, the first faces and points of contact the public encounters in the courthouse. They began to see their jobs and responsibilities expand beyond what happens between nine and five. The folks coming through the court represent their neighbors; if court employees want to live better, their neighbors have to be healthier and enjoy an improved quality of life. Not to mention the gratification of having a global impact on justice.

The courthouse can also become a place that offers assistance to staff members themselves, like the court attendant who brings his father, a veteran, to our courthouse for the monthly veterans' counseling day. He began doing so after observing veterans who had been denied benefits by Veterans Affairs obtain them through the court. After working with a counselor, his father now receives the assistance and benefits he is entitled to.

I also saw my work's impact when I was invited to the Obama White House with 150 others from across the country for a convening on criminal justice reform. The group included US attorneys, state supreme court chief justices, defense attorneys, legislators, representatives of nonprofit organizations, and formerly incarcerated individuals. I was asked to facilitate a conversation during a lunch session. During the question-and-answer period at the end of the event, an attorney remarked, "It's like Judge Pratt said. . . ." I've heard audience members open their sentences this way after every panel or conference where I've spoken. I've heard it so often that I started using it as a hashtag: #JudgePrattSaid. People repeating my words means not only that they listened but that the content resonated with them.

I felt the impact when I was approached by new police officers who recognized me from my TED Talk about procedural justice, which is shown to cadets at the police academy in New Jersey. "Judge, I saw your talk during my training at the academy. Thank you so much for giving me another approach," a Newark officer said after I had performed a wedding she happened to be attending. She just wanted to show appreciation. As I was walking across the street one day, another Newark police officer turned and yelled, "Your video was great! I saw it at the academy, and I use all those steps while I'm out here."

The use of my TED Talk as a training tool at the police academy provides cadets with the principles of fairness as a foundation for their understanding of their profession and role. Being introduced to the principles early in their training increases the likelihood that they will assimilate and practice them as officers. It is certainly more effective than relying on training that emphasizes military-style policing and having to retrofit the ideals of humanity and respect into officers' work as a late-arriving correction.

Justice is not only about deciding who is good and who is bad, who is worthy and who is unworthy, who is safe and who is dangerous. The punitive model applied in the United States is extreme, but it is not the global norm. Twenty years ago the Norwegian government decided to overhaul its prison system. It imposes no life sentences, so there is a presumption that the incarcerated will return to society. Prisoners are offered all-day educational and training activities. Correctional officers are required to serve as motivators and mentors in those sessions. Prisoners are prepared to be good neighbors when they are released. This approach has led to Norway's having one of the lowest recidivism rates in the world.[1]

It also demonstrates a broader vision of how a justice system can operate: instead of taking on a primary role of division and separation, it can heal, restore, and strengthen communities. To have healthy communities, we must dismantle biased and destructive social and economic structures. We must create opportunities where everyone can make a meaningful contribution.

This is one of the many ideas I want to pass on to you and to the community as a whole. You are inseparably connected to your fellow citizens. You lose the potential value of your neighbors' contributions if they are not living at their full potential. If they live in poverty, you are less wealthy. If they perpetually cycle through the criminal justice system, you will lose neighbors and friends, and your community will be full of broken families and friendships. And for you, son, as an African American and Latino male, the suffering of your peers puts you in peril by providing a stronghold for continued racism and discrimination. Therefore, we must identify the factors within our institutions, our policies, and our actions that keep our neighbors subjugated. Then we must correct them.

Criminal justice practitioners often remain suspended in this hallucination that what is happening to members of marginalized and underserved communities is justice. We know it is not. To have the greatest impact on reforming our systems, I can make two recommendations.

Embrace a Radically Human Approach to Justice

We must not be constrained by orthodox behaviors that impede the delivery of justice. A radical approach merely requires a reframing of that which is usual or customary. I'm asking people to deviate from their typical patterns. People, however, often respond to new concepts the way the body responds to infection: they attack it.

To achieve the goal of radical humanity, people must undergo a paradigm shift. In his book *The 7 Habits of Highly Effective People*, Stephen R. Covey writes, "We see the world not as it is, but as we are—or, as we are conditioned to see it."[2] Paradigms are the patterns we anticipate, our perceptions of how things are. Too often, people presume that the word "defendant" or "suspect" is synonymous with "guilty person." Their treatment of the individual's case is then framed by this perception. Perceptions determine outcomes. We need to shift the usual practices so that we can truly uphold the principle of the presumption of innocence. That should guide how we treat people during the entire judicial process.

A radically human approach also requires us to discard antiquated paradigms that don't align with fairness. A broad-minded, progressive approach to justice must extend to how police officers and prosecutors determine what charges to impose. The practice of overcharging defendants must end. Overcharging entails including criminal charges the state can't prove—that is, throwing everything at the defendant but the kitchen sink, so to speak. Overcharging gives the state an advantage during plea negotiations.

The radically human approach also requires that we invest in treating people with dignity and respect. These values must be priorities when engaging those who come through the system—even when we encounter them in other circumstances. Focusing on these values is how we increase the public's trust in us and connect with the people we serve. Not to mention that we enhance the possibility of being seen as legitimate authorities.

The justice system compels individuals—who are innocent until proven guilty—to report to the courthouse and respond to allegations. Punishing them with an overly difficult process for following these rules *before* a finding of guilt or innocence has been made is unjust and causes significant harm. Guilt or innocence has become an afterthought.

We can demonstrate dignity and respect in how we communicate with individuals. It is critical to listen to them intentionally with the purpose of understanding and seeing them beyond their circumstances. We must apply new strategies if we want outcomes that are fair and that promote justice. We need to approach all decisions in a way that respects members of the community.

Pursue a Multifaceted Approach to Justice

Truly reforming the criminal justice system requires innovation, partnership, and courage. Innovation needs to come in various forms, such as alternative sentencing or tailoring justice to meet the needs of the individual and the community. The system also needs to expand its mission to address individuals' underlying social needs.

The system must move away from a cookie-cutter approach to justice, which is not merely dehumanizing and reductive; it allows for bias and leads to unfair outcomes. A broader, multifaceted approach allows the system to work toward rehabilitation as early as the moment of arrest. And rehabilitation needs to be offered as an alternative to jail or prison.

In the court system in which I served, partnerships among Newark Community Solutions, community members, nonprofit organizations, faith-based organizations, and others who cared about the criminal justice system proved crucial. These stakeholders were central in providing services to support innovation. Most importantly, they were invaluable in the rehabilitation and reintegration of defendants into society. It is necessary and prudent for justice practitioners to collaborate with people who have been doing other kinds of community work.

Reform requires courage. Young man, we have a responsibility to say "Ouch" when someone steps on our toes. That means you cannot stay silent when someone's actions cause you or others harm. Collectively, we must not be afraid to address wrongdoing or injustice. Identifying those harms allows people and institutions to engage in discourse about the issue and to take corrective action.

Please note, you have a greater responsibility to bring attention to injustice when you are on the side that causes it. As an African American and Latina judge, I have been a part of the system, shouting about why we need to change, where we need to change, and the urgency of that change. Still, I often feel as though I'm not doing enough. Traveling across the country speaking to judges, their staff prosecutors, public defenders, and law enforcement officers, I wonder how to reach them all. Add to that a TED Talk with millions of views, and it still does not seem adequate. Traveling and speaking to people globally about improving justice—still not enough. During this tumultuous time in our country's history, I too often feel powerless.

However, I know that doing nothing is the real crime.

In the end, we must be brave enough to persevere. We have to be willing to take on initiatives that get to the heart of the matter. If we want to keep children out of jail and prison, if we want to keep families together and communities prospering, we are responsible for providing solutions to the problems we see around us. That also means we have to be in the business of being preemptive, of taking preventive action.

Courage is necessary when you try something new. When faced with a challenge, you need to innovate solutions. When someone has caused harm, when their unlawful behavior is tearing at the fabric of a community, they must be deterred and guided out of that behavior. This doesn't mean casting them out of society for making a mistake. Some people need support, and we can focus community resources on those entrenched in the trouble we are attempting to prevent. Some of these folks are the most vulnerable among us—the impoverished, the mentally ill, the traumatized. Restoring them so they can contribute to society may take effort, but the rewards to the community can last a lifetime.

Burying our heads in the sand will not help us avoid or correct the catastrophic and far-reaching effects of overincarceration. We ask folks to make better choices when there are often no choices to be made at all. This is not a statement in support of lawlessness. It is, however, a comment about what happens when we don't make the criminal justice system serve the needs of the community. A society's true values can be seen in how it treats the most vulnerable and marginalized.

The lessons I have learned from the bench have been considerable, but they are just the tip of the iceberg. Looking at people with a fresh perspective means seeing them as our country's most valuable resources. We must believe that people are redeemable. We can expand our commitment to justice by moving beyond preconceived notions about who is reformable and who isn't, who has worth and who doesn't. We cannot continue to ignore the vulnerable and the predicaments they are in simply because they make bad decisions. Instead, we must make a conscious effort to assist them. We have to see potential in everyone's life, especially in the lives of the most marginalized.

My goal is to leave a legacy of love and respect, and a message that we need to see possibility in all people. I want people in authority to understand that it is their responsibility to help reform our institutions. In fact, they need to know that they already have the ability to facilitate that transformation. We are entrusted with leaving things better than we found them.

I want the courthouse to become more than a place where people pay fines or end up when they are in trouble. Instead, I want it to be a place that helps folks unravel the problem that landed them there. A place that gives them resources to navigate other agencies, but also a place that plays a part in eradicating poverty and supporting communities.

Son, we live in a country where racial injustice persists, and that has to end. Addressing it often feels like an impossible uphill battle. So I swallow hard, pray harder, think of you, and get back to work. And improving the criminal justice system and raising you into an extraordinary human being are the contributions that I've been called to make.

I want these words to make you feel full of hope, full of love, full of concern for your fellow citizen. I want them to fill you with intellectual curiosity. I want them to illuminate the corners in your life and make you feel powerful. I want you to know that you are a blessing and can have anything you want in life. I want you to live in a world where you are free to jump, climb, explore, and discover. I want you to live this way without having to pull you back out of fear that this is a dangerous place for Black children.

Dr. Martin Luther King Jr. once said, "There comes a time when one must take a position that is neither safe, nor politic, nor popular, but he must take it because conscience tells him it is right."

When your time comes, you will be ready.

Love you always hijo de mi alma,
Mama

AUTHOR'S NOTE

I have changed the names of all those who appeared before me, and of some others discussed in the book, as well as some of their identifying details, to protect their privacy. Others have asked to have their actual names and identities included.

I have retold these stories as they occurred, or based on how they were recounted to me, to the best of my recollection. While it was impossible to fact-check every detail of the stories related here, I did not include stories that I did not believe to be true.

ACKNOWLEDGMENTS

Writing this book was one of the most significant challenges of my life. And like all great achievements, I did not do it alone.

First, to the Almighty God, thank you for allowing me to be an instrument of your work and permitting me to serve those that you have put in my path. I am so grateful that you continue to honor my mother's prayers for my life, even in her physical absence.

To my loving husband, Paul Lucien, for speaking this book up on our first encounter. Thank you for never being surprised when I exceed my own expectations. Your love has made all the difference in my life. I love you dearly.

To my gift from God, my son, Hendrick, I hope this book leaves the world a better place for you to have a future.

Thank you to my mother, Elsa, whose example is responsible for any good and any innovation that I have done in my life. Thank you to Allan, my father, for giving me more love, more hope, and more understanding than you ever received in life. And thank you to my wonderful brother, Allen Pratt Jr., for your beautiful and generous spirit and for supporting me throughout this process, and every other endeavor, including by watching your nephew.

I am eternally grateful to my extraordinary editor, the indomitable Emi Ikkanda, who quickly saw the potential for this project. Thank you for taking a chance on me and helping bring these stories to life. To you and the Seal Press publishing team, without whom *The Power of Dignity* would not exist, thank you for supporting and encouraging me through this crazy ride!

To my brilliant research assistant, Tiana Mills, I am indebted to you for your keen insight, honesty, and probing questions all along the way.

While I know he doesn't like to hear it, I'm eternally grateful to my beloved uncle Claude Trahan. Without his encouragement, I never would have completed this project.

To the wise sage Denis Gooding, for the countless conversations that helped flesh out ideas in this book. Your contribution was invaluable.

To Dr. Ansley Lamar, my life coach and my friend since Toastmasters. Thank you for those weekly writing meetings. Without them, I would never have gotten the book proposal done. I am so grateful.

To my friend and brother Jethro Antoine, Esq., thank you for your willingness to brainstorm this project early on in my career and for insisting I keep a journal. And to Greg Berman, to whom I am forever grateful for reading early drafts, giving me indispensable feedback, and listening to me complain the whole time. Thank you both for your innovation, vision for Newark, and commitment to these ideas.

To the Center for Court Innovation, with a special shout out to Courtney Bryan, Matt Watkins, Robert Wolf, Bill Harkins, and Anna Pomper, and all the employees whose dedication and expertise were crucial to this project and to improving justice everywhere.

To my remarkable literary agent, Mel Berger of WME, the grand poobah of literary agents. I so appreciate you for taking me on as a client and your relentless work to bring this book to print. And to my agent, the incredible Henry Reisch of WME, thank you for hearing my message and devising a plan to get it out into the world.

I am forever grateful to my judicial dream team: Judge Dion Williams, for being my first judicial coach and an example of decency; Judge Bahir Kamil, for your sage wisdom while coaching me through the Deuce; Judge Julien Neals, for being my sponsor, brother, and friend; the discerning Judge Richard Nunes, for entrusting me with an assignment to the Community Court; Judge Harold Fullilove II, for insisting I pursue the job and supporting me; and the incomparable Justice Fern Fisher, for always pointing me in the right direction.

To my amazing bridal gang, Dr. Nyeema Watson, Alberta Stewart, Esq., Camilia Valdes, Esq., Marsha Moore, Esq., Walda Laurenceau, and Richelle Claiborne. I would not have had the wherewithal to get through this and my other life challenges without you all cheering me on. I love you, my sisters.

A very special thanks to Anton Lendor, Esq., Aliya King Neil, Larry Crump, Esq., Ali McBride, and Bernarda Grullon, who saw the idea for this book years ago and harassed me relentlessly about it. Blessed to have you all lifting me up.

To Audrey Grant and Stacey Gatlin Harley for keeping me lifted in prayer and being great at the things I'm terrible at, so this project could get done.

Senator Cory Booker for including me in and trusting me with your vision for justice in Newark and for truly being a big brother in my journey in Newark Municipal Court.

Congressman Donald Payne, for your friendship and dogged persistence in advancing women, especially me, no matter what obstacles appear.

Modia Butler, thank you for never flinching or backing down when it came to getting me on the bench. You'll never know how much I truly appreciate your faith in me.

Mayor Ras Baraka, thank you for practicing what you preach and inviting me into your plan for the city of Newark by making me the chief judge.

To my friend and mentor Lance McPherson, Esq., for all the legal and career advice, help, and encouragement to get here.

I am forever grateful to the Part Two staff and crew for ensuring that the magic happened every day: Alethia Parker, Ivonne Bowers, Beverly Anderson, Maurice Rodwell, Ronald High, Mark Lunger, Judge Ashley Gibbons, Judge Vivian Sanks King, Ismael Castro, Onya Harris, Derek Graham, Christine Victor, Officer Mickey Carillo, Sgt. Jon Henriquez, Officer Michael Blount, Earline Holt, Officer Marion Salome, Officer Najee Webb, Officer Albert Cosgrove, Herbert Washington, Esq., Albert Mrozik, Esq., Evans Anyanwu, and Toya Gavin, Esq. Thanks again for allowing me to push you and for embracing this cultural shift.

A special thanks to Officer Mickey Carillo for having my back on this crusade and allowing us to see what true policing can really be.

To my attorney, Darrell Miller, Esq., thank you for all the legal and spiritual insights.

To the best big sisters ever, Jada Bookhart, Leslie Peters, Sonja Clark, Christine Palms, Sandra Mazara Wheeler, Dionne Wynn, Dr. Bonnie Vesey, and Dr. Hortensia Kelly. Thank you for never hesitating when I'm in need and for your unwavering love and support throughout this process and in my life.

To Philip Thomas and Andre Taylor, thank you for always filling my head with ideas larger than life and then pushing me to make them a reality.

My most heartfelt gratitude to Mama Rosalyn Sugihara, Tia Elsa Davis, Dr. Carl McGloster, Ken Louis, Angelica Ogando, Rosa Del Valle, Patricia Hernandez, Ryan Haygood, Esq., and Cherise Foster for the continuous support, love, and encouragement that made this book a reality.

A profound thanks to the entire Newark Community Solutions staff for fighting for justice for the people you serve every day.

To Tina Rosenberg, I am forever grateful to you for putting our work in Newark on the world stage by featuring it in your *Guardian* article. Thank you so much for being so committed to finding solutions to society's problems.

To Council President Mildred Crump, thank you for teaching me what it means to be a faithful public servant. For voting to make Newark's Community Solutions a reality, I would like to thank the Newark Municipal Council, Council President Mildred Crump, Councilman Carlos Gonzalez, Councilman Anibal Ramos, Councilman Luis Quintana, Councilman Oscar James Jr., Councilman Augusto Amador, Councilman Ronald Rice Jr., and Councilwoman Dana Rone.

I am beyond grateful to Ms. Lola, Ms. Nina, Titi Carmen Perez, and Ms. Rose Cordoba for taking such amazing care of my gift from God, Hendrick, that I was allowed to write, knowing he was in good hands.

To my awesome nieces and goddaughters, Celia, Olivia, Kailee, Zora, Nyeri, Cheyenne, Amber, JayJay, Benee, Tempest, Athena, Jade, Elsa, Isabella, Angelique, Margarite, Lizbeth, Katherine, Tianna, and Zuri. Thank you for being my inspiration.

A special note of gratitude to the TED team Chris Anderson, Kelly Stoetzel, Cloe Shasha, and David Biello for inviting me to share my message with the world and championing my cause.

To the entire Newark Community Solutions staff, whose love and commitment make make magic happen. Thank you!

I am indebted to all the people who came through my court and were willing to open up their hearts and lives to me—there are too many to name. Thank you for helping me grow by making me listen, learn, see, and check my ego.

To my other family, friends, Newark Municipal Court family, and Rutgers University SCJ and Rutgers Law Newark colleagues who continue to support me endlessly, I am forever grateful.

NOTES

Introduction

1. US Department of Justice, Civil Rights Division, *Investigation of the Newark Police Department* (2014), www.justice.gov/sites/default/files /crt/legacy/2014/07/22/newark_findings_7-22-14.pdf.

2. Erika Harrell and Elizabeth Davis, *Contacts Between Police and the Public, 2018—Statistical Tables*, report no. 255730 (US Department of Justice, Bureau of Justice Statistics, 2020), https://bjs.ojp.gov/content /pub/pdf/cbpp18st.pdf.

Chapter 1: A Better Approach

1. Doris A. Fuller et al., *Overlooked in the Undercounted: The Role of Mental Illness in Fatal Law Enforcement Encounters* (Treatment Advocacy Center, 2015), www.treatmentadvocacycenter.org/overlooked-in-the -undercounted.

2. "People Killed in 2016," *The Guardian*, www.theguardian.com /us-news/ng-interactive/2015/jun/01/the-counted-police-killings-us -database.

3. Rich Morin and Renee Stepler, *The Racial Confidence Gap in Police Performance* (Washington, DC: Pew Research Center, 2016).

4. Tom R. Tyler, *Why People Obey the Law*, rev. ed. (Princeton, NJ: Princeton University Press, 2006).

5. Malcolm Gladwell, *David and Goliath: Underdogs, Misfits, and the Art of Battling Giants* (New York: Back Bay Books, 2015), 207–208.

6. Tyler, *Why People Obey the Law.*

7. Greg Berman and Emily Gold, "Procedural Justice from the Bench: How Judges Can Improve the Effectiveness of Criminal Courts," *Judges' Journal* 51, no. 2 (Spring 2012).

8. "Forcing Black Men Out of Society," editorial, *New York Times*, April 25, 2015, www.nytimes.com/2015/04/26/opinion/sunday/forcing-black-men-out-of-society.html; Stephanie R. Bush-Baskette, *Misguided Justice: The War on Drugs and the Incarceration of Black Women* (self-published: iUniverse, 2010).

9. Brett Johnson, "N.J. Supreme Court Says Judges Broke Rules by Dining with Indicted Friend," NJ.com, updated March 29, 2019, www.nj.com/politics/2015/01/nj_supreme_court_does_not_punish_judges_who_died_with_indicted_friend.html.

10. New Jersey Courts, *Veterans Assistance Project* (2018), www.njcourts.gov/forms/12007_vets_assist_state_web.pdf.

11. State v. Johnson, 67 New Jersey Superior Court Reports (Superior Court of New Jersey Appellate Division, May 5, 1961).

12. S. M. Carey, J. R. Mackin, and M. W. Finigan, "What Works? The Ten Key Components of Drug Court: Research-Based Best Practices," *Drug Court Review* 8, no. 1 (2012).

Chapter 2: I Hear You

1. Ralph G. Nichols, "The Struggle to Be Human," keynote address, First Annual Convention of the International Listening Association, February 17, 1980, www.listen.org/resources/Documents/Nichols%20Struggle%20to%20be%20Human.pdf.

2. Martin Luther King Jr., with a foreword by Coretta Scott King, and a new foreword by Raphael G. Warnock, *A Gift of Love: Sermons from Strength to Love and Other Preachings* (London: Penguin, 2017).

3. Emily J. Ross et al., "Developmental Consequences of Fetal Exposure to Drugs: What We Know and What We Still Must Learn," *Neuropsychopharmacology* 40, no. 1 (July 30, 2014).

4. Malika Saada Saar et al., *The Sexual Abuse to Prison Pipeline: The Girls' Story* (Washington, DC: Georgetown Law Center on Poverty and Inequality, 2019).

5. Wendy Sawyer, "Youth Confinement: The Whole Pie 2019," Prison Policy Initiative, December 19, 2019, www.prisonpolicy.org /reports/youth2019.html.

6. Saada Saar et al., *The Sexual Abuse to Prison Pipeline.*

7. Kiese Laymon, *How to Slowly Kill Yourself and Others in America* (Evanston, IL: Agate Bolden, 2013).

Chapter 3: I See You

1. Deborah M. Stone, Christopher M. Jones, and Karin A. Mack, "Changes in Suicide Rates—United States, 2018–2019," *Morbidity and Mortality Weekly Report* 70, no. 8 (February 26, 2021).

2. American Association of Suicidology, "African American Suicide Fact Sheet Based on 2014 Data," 2016, www.wellspacehealth .org/wp-content/uploads/2016/10/African-American-Suicide-Fact -Sheet-2016.pdf.

3. Sidney H. Hankerson, Derek Suite, and Rahn K. Bailey, "Treatment Disparities Among African American Men with Depression: Implications for Clinical Practice," *Journal of Health Care for the Poor and Underserved* 26, no. 1 (April 22, 2015).

4. Cynthia G. Lee et al., *A Community Court Grows in Brooklyn: A Comprehensive Evaluation of the Red Hook Community Justice Center* (New York: Center for Court Innovation, 2012).

5. Maria C. Mancebo et al., "Substance Use Disorders in an Obsessive Compulsive Disorder Clinical Sample," *Journal of Anxiety Disorders* 23, no. 4 (May 2009).

6. Address by Rabbi Joachim Prinz, President of the American Jewish Congress, at the March on Washington for Jobs and Freedom, Lincoln Memorial, August 28, 1963, PC-3551, the Jacob Rader Marcus Center of American Jewish Archives, Cincinnati, Ohio.

7. "The 50th Anniversary of Martin Luther King, Jr.'s 'What Is Your Life's Blueprint?,'" Beacon Broadside: A Project of Beacon Press, October 26, 2017, www.beaconbroadside.com/broadside/2017/10/the -50th-anniversary-of-martin-luther-king-jrs-what-is-your-lifes-blue print.html.

8. National Judicial College, "8 More Mistakes New Judges Often Make—and How to Avoid Them," Judges.org, last modified August 16, 2018, www.judges.org/news-and-info/8-more-mistakes -new-judges-often-make-and-how-to-avoid-them/.

Chapter 4: Poverty Is Not a Crime

1. Population Research Institute, "Episode 4: Poverty: Where We All Started," overpopulationisamyth.com, accessed August 12, 2021, https://overpopulationisamyth.com/episode-4-poverty-where-we-all-started/.

2. Mary E. Fairhurst, "Welcoming Remarks to New Bar Admittees," *Seattle Journal for Social Justice* 4, no. 2 (May 2006).

3. Lucius Couloute, "Getting Back on Course: Educational Exclusion and Attainment Among Formerly Incarcerated People," Prison Policy Initiative, 2018, www.prisonpolicy.org/reports/education.html.

4. US Department of Justice, Civil Rights Division, *Investigation of the Ferguson Police Department* (March 4, 2015), www.justice.gov/sites/default/files/opa/press-releases/attachments/2015/03/04/ferguson_police_department_report.pdf.

5. US Department of Justice, *Investigation of the Ferguson Police Department*.

6. Terry-Ann Craigie et al., *Conviction, Imprisonment, and Lost Earnings: How Involvement with the Criminal Justice System Deepens Inequality* (New York: Brennan Center for Justice, 2020), www.brennancenter.org/our-work/research-reports/conviction-imprisonment-and-lost-earnings-how-involvement-criminal.

7. Azadeh Zohrabi et al., *Who Pays?: The True Cost of Incarceration on Families* (Oakland, CA: Ella Baker Center, Forward Together, Research Action Design, 2015), http://whopaysreport.org/wp-content/uploads/2015/09/Who-Pays-FINAL.pdf.

8. V. J. Felitti et al., "Relationship of Childhood Abuse and Household Dysfunction to Many of the Leading Causes of Death in Adults: The Adverse Childhood Experiences (ACE) Study," *American Journal of Preventive Medicine* 14, no. 4 (1998).

Chapter 5: Reforms That Transform

1. Greg Berman and John Feinblatt, with Sarah Glazer, *Good Courts: The Case for Problem-Solving Justice* (New York: New Press, 2005).

2. Stephanie R. Bush-Baskette, *Misguided Justice: The War on Drugs and the Incarceration of Black Women* (self-published: iUniverse, 2010).

3. Mayo Clinic, "Kleptomania," last modified October 21, 2017, www.mayoclinic.org/diseases-conditions/kleptomania/symptoms-causes/syc-20364732.

Chapter 6: Transforming the Justice System

1. George L. Kelling and James Q. Satchell, "Broken Windows: The Police and Neighborhood Safety," *The Atlantic*, March 1982.

2. Malika Saada Saar et al., *The Sexual Abuse to Prison Pipeline: The Girls' Story* (Washington, DC: Georgetown Law Center on Poverty and Inequality, 2019).

3. Lama Hassoun Ayoub et al., *School Discipline, Safety, and Climate: A Comprehensive Study in New York City* (New York: Center for Court Innovation, 2019), www.courtinnovation.org/school-discipline.

4. Howard Zehr, *The Little Book of Restorative Justice: Revised and Updated* (New York: Good Books, 2015), 48.

5. "What Is Cognitive Behavioral Therapy?," American Psychological Association, last modified July 2017, www.apa.org/ptsd-guideline /patients-and-families/cognitive-behavioral.

6. "APA Policy: Applied Behavior Analysis," American Psychological Association, last modified February 2017, www.apa.org/about /policy/applied-behavior-analysis.

7. William Wical, Joseph Richardson, and Che Bullock, "A Credible Messenger: The Role of the Violence Intervention Specialist in the Lives of Young Black Male Survivors of Violence," *Violence and Gender* 7, no. 2 (June 12, 2020), http://doi.org/10.1089/vio.2019.0026.

8. Rich Morin and Renee Stepler, *The Racial Confidence Gap in Police Performance* (Washington, DC: Pew Research Center, 2016).

9. Melissa Bradley et al., "Procedural Justice: A Training Model for Organizational-Level Change," *Police Chief Magazine*, accessed August 11, 2021, www.policechiefmagazine.org/procedural-justice-a-training -model-for-organizational-level-change/.

10. Megan Quattlebaum, Tracey Meares, and Tom Tyler, *Principles of Procedurally Just Policing* (Justice Collaboratory at Yale Law School, January 2018), https://law.yale.edu/sites/default/files/area/center/justice /principles_of_procedurally_just_policing_report.pdf.

11. Norma M. Riccucci, Gregg G. Van Ryzin, and Cecilia F. Lavena, "Representative Bureaucracy in Policing: Does It Increase Perceived Legitimacy?," *Journal of Public Administration Research and Theory* 24, no. 3 (July 2014), https://doi.org/10.1093/jopart/muu006.

12. Boscar A. Ba et al., "The Role of Officer Race and Gender in Police-Civilian Interactions in Chicago," *Science*, February 12, 2021.

13. Amie M. Schuck and Cara Rabe-Hemp, "Women Police: The Use of Force By and Against Female Officers," *Women and Criminal Justice* 16, no. 4 (2005).

14. Women's Leadership Academy, home page, accessed August 13, 2021, www.womensleadpd.org/.

15. Alana Semuels, "Society Is Paying the Price for America's Outdated Police Training Methods," *Time*, November 20, 2020, https://time.com/5901726/police-training-academies/.

16. Randy Shrewsberry, "Former Police Officer Says Training Methods for Cops Need to Change," interview with Debbie Elliott, *Weekend Edition Saturday*, April 17, 2021, www.npr.org/2021/04/17/988331517/former-police-officer-says-training-methods-for-cops-need-to-change.

17. Thomas C. O'Brien and Tom R. Tyler, "Rebuilding Trust Between Police and Communities Through Procedural Justice and Reconciliation," *Behavioral Science and Policy* 5, no. 1 (2019).

18. Brent Woodie, "Violent Crime Up in Major US Cities Since Covid-19 Pandemic Began," *Route Fifty*, June 2, 2021, www.route-fifty.com/public-safety/2021/06/report-violent-crime-spiked-major-us-cities-covid-19-pandemic-began/174461/.

19. Quattlebaum, Meares, and Tyler, *Principles of Procedurally Just Policing.*

20. US Department of Justice, Office of Community Oriented Policing Services, *Final Report of the President's Task Force on 21st Century Policing* (Washington, DC, 2015).

21. O'Brien and Tyler, "Rebuilding Trust," 35–50.

Chapter 7: Reformed Leadership

1. CBSNews.com Staff, "The Delinquents: A Spate of Rhino Killings," *CBS News*, August 22, 2000, www.cbsnews.com/news/the-delinquents/.

2. Greg Berman and John Feinblatt, with Sarah Glazer, *Good Courts: The Case for Problem-Solving Justice* (New York: New Press, 2005).

3. Kerrin C. Wolf and Aaron Kupchik, "School Suspensions and Adverse Experiences in Adulthood," *Justice Quarterly* 34, no. 3 (2017).